For the Love of cakes

Publisher's Note:
Raw or semi-cooked eggs should not be consumed by babies, toddlers, pregnant or breastfeeding women, the elderly or those suffering from a chronic illness.

Publisher & Creative Director: Nick Wells
Senior Project Editor: Catherine Taylor
Editorial: Laura Bulbeck
Art Director: Mike Spender
Layout Design: Jane Ashley
Digital Design & Production: Chris Herbert

Special thanks to Charlotte McLean, Digby Smith and Helen Wall.

This is a FLAME TREE book

FLAME TREE PUBLISHING

Crabtree Hall, Crabtree Lane
Fulham, London SW6 6TY
United Kingdom
www.flametreepublishing.com

Flame Tree is part of The Foundry Creative Media Company Limited

First published 2011

11 13 15 14 12
1 3 5 7 9 10 8 6 4 2

ISBN: 978-0-85775-258-1

A copy of the CIP data for this book is available from the British Library.

Printed in China

For the Love of cakes

General Editor: Gina Steer

FLAME TREE
PUBLISHING

Contents

Introduction

Cakes have long been part of celebrations in various forms, as well as being considered delicious treats for more informal times. Home baking offers the opportunity to whip up both easy-to-make cakes and slightly more sophisticated offerings, in various shapes and sizes.

Home-made cakes are cheaper than shop-bought cakes, quick and easy to make and provide delicious treats, as well as being great for birthdays, Christmas or other celebrations. There is no comparison to the quality of home-made cakes and the fun to be had in making them. Children love to get involved in baking cakes, which provides a fun and creative family activity. Baking and decorating yourself also means you can personalise them for whatever the occasion and cater for your personal preference. This book has a wide range of recipes, some very quick and easy, some requiring a little more patience.

Another advantage of making your own cakes is that you can control which ingredients you use, thus ensuring that none of the ingredients will trigger any allergies.

This book will show you how easy it is to make and bake cakes and you will find many different varieties to try, from classic sponges to loaf cakes and cupcakes. By following the advice from preparation to decoration, you will discover for yourself how rewarding it is to taste and show off a cake you have made yourself!

Using This Book

This book is aimed at showing both the occasional and well-practised baker how to create delicious cakes, both for special occasions and simply for an afternoon treat. The recipes in this book are divided into handy categories,

covering everyday cakes, chocolate cakes and special occasion and dessert cakes for when you want to entertain or make something really special. By reading the guide to equipment and ingredients at the front of the book, as well as decoration tips, baking cakes will be made much easier and result in success far more often.

The essential cake baking ingredients are discussed, covering the varying types of fat, flour, eggs and sugar. Basic but important techniques such as how to line cake tins correctly and different methods of mixing are covered, and once mastered will help build your confidence in baking. We then go on to look at the various ways to decorate your cakes, including a section dedicated to handling chocolate.

First read through the advice at the beginning of this book, and then have a go at choosing a recipe which looks good to you. The best idea is to read the recipe through thoroughly and then assemble and measure out all the ingredients you will need. Preheating your oven will also ensure that your cake will cook to its best.

Measuring

The recipes contained in this book offer both metric and imperial measurements, but as they are not exact equivalents it is essential to stick to one set of measurements. All spoon measurements should be used level for accuracy, and always use a recognised set of spoon measures for best results. Ensuring that the ingredients are accurately measured is vital for baking success, therefore a good set of kitchen scales for solids and measuring jugs for liquids are very important. A cake that has too much flour or insufficient egg will be dry and crumbly. Too much raising agent will mean that the cake will rise too quickly and then sink. Insufficient raising agent means the cake will not rise in the first place.

Using Your Oven

Ensure that the oven is preheated to the correct temperature; it can take 10 minutes to reach 180°C/350°F/Gas Mark 4. You may find that an oven thermometer is a good investment. Cakes are best if cooked in the centre of the preheated oven. Try to avoid opening the oven door at the start of cooking as a draught can make the cake sink. If using a fan oven you will need to reduce the temperature stated in the recipe by 10 per cent, which is usually 20°C. Check that the cake is thoroughly cooked by removing from the oven and inserting a clean skewer. Leave for 30 seconds and remove. If clean then the cake is cooked, if there is a little mixture return to the oven for a few minutes.

Avoiding Problems

When you take your cake out of the oven, unless the recipe states that it should be left in the tin until cold, leave for a few minutes, then loosen the edges and turn out on to a wire rack to cool. Cakes which are left in the tin for too long, tend to sink or slightly overcook. When storing, make sure the cake is completely cold before placing it into an airtight tin or plastic container.

Other problems encountered during cake making are insufficient creaming of the fat and sugar or a curdled mixture (which will result in a fairly solid cake). Flour that has not been folded in carefully enough or has not been mixed with enough raising agent may also result in a fairly heavy consistency. Be aware – especially when cooking with fruit – that if the consistency is too soft, the cake will not be able to support the fruit. Ensure that the correct size of tin is used as you may end up either with a flat, hard cake or one which has spilled over the edge of the tin.

Equipment and Utensils

Cooking equipment not only assists in the kitchen, but can make all the difference between success and failure. Take the humble cake tin, although a very basic piece of cooking equipment, it plays an essential role in baking. Using a tin that is too large will spread the mixture too thinly and the result will be a flat, limp-looking cake. On the other hand, cramming the mixture into a tin which is too small will result in the mixture rising up and out of the tin.

Bakeware

To ensure successful baking it is worth investing in a selection of high quality tins, which, if looked after properly, should last for many years. Follow the manufacturers' instructions when first using and ensure that the tins are thoroughly washed and dried after use and before putting away.

Sandwich Cake Tins

Perhaps the most useful of tins for baking are sandwich cake tins, ideal for classics such as Victoria sponge cake. You will need two tins and they are normally 18 cm/7 inches or 20.5 cm/8 inches in diameter and are about 5–7.5cm/2–3 inches deep and often nonstick.

Deep Cake Tins

With deep cake tins, it is personal choice whether you buy round or square tins. They vary in size from 12.5–35.5 cm/5–14 inches with a depth of between 12.5–15 cm/5–6 inches. A deep cake tin, for everyday fruit or Madeira cake is a must, a useful size is 20.5 cm/8 inches.

Loaf Tins

Loaf tins come in two sizes, 450 g/1 lb and 900 g/2 lb.

Other Tins

There are plenty of other tins to choose from, ranging from themed and shaped tins, such as Christmas trees, numbers and petals, to ring mould tins (tins with a hole in the centre) and springform tins where the sides release after cooking, allowing the finished cake to be removed easily. A selection of different sized roasting tins is also a worthwhile investment as they can double up as a bain-marie, or for cooking larger quantities of cakes such as gingerbread.

Other Essential Items

Mixing bowls

Three to four different sizes of mixing bowls are also very useful for mixing and melting ingredients.

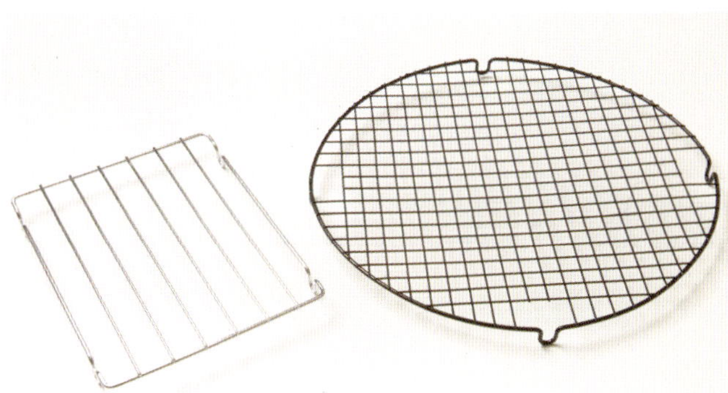

Wire Cooling Racks

Another essential piece of equipment is a wire cooling rack. It is essential when baking to allow cakes to cool after being removed from their tins. A wire rack also protects your kitchen surfaces from the heat and allows air to circulate around the goodies, speeding cooling and preventing soggy bottoms.

Scales and Cutlery

Baking needs 100 per cent accuracy to ensure a perfect result. Scales come in many shapes and sizes, both digital and with weights. Most have a weigh pan although, with some, your own bowl is used. Measuring jugs and spoons are essential for accurate measuring of both dry and wet ingredients. Basic mixing cutlery is also essential, such as a wooden spoon (for mixing and creaming), a spatula (for transferring the mixture from the mixing bowl to the baking tins and spreading the mixture once it is in the tins) and a palette knife (to ease cakes out of their tins before placing them on the wire racks to cool).

Electrical Equipment

Nowadays help from time-saving gadgets and electrical equipment makes baking far easier and quicker. Equipment can be used for creaming, mixing, beating, whisking, grating and chopping. There is a wide choice of machines available from the most basic to the highly sophisticated.

Food Processors

First decide what you need your processor to do when choosing a machine. If you are a novice to baking, it may be a waste to start with a machine which offers a wide range of implements and functions. This can be off-putting and result in not using the machine to its ultimate.

When buying a food processor look for measurements on the side of the processor bowl and machines with a removable feed tube which allows food or liquid to be added while the motor is still running. Look out for machines that have the facility to increase the capacity of the bowl and have a pulse button for controlled chopping. For many, storage is an issue so reversible discs and flex storage, or on more advanced models, a blade storage compartment or box, can be advantageous.

It is also worth thinking about machines which offer optional extras which can be bought as your cooking requirements change. Mini-chopping bowls are available for those wanting to chop small quantities of food. If time is an issue, dishwasher-friendly attachments may be vital. Citrus presses, liquidisers and whisks may all be useful attachments for the individual cook.

Blenders

Blenders often come as attachments to food processors and are generally used for liquidising and purééing foods. There are two main types of blender. The first is known as a goblet blender. The blades of this blender are at the bottom of the goblet with measurements up the sides. The second blender is portable. It is hand-held and should be placed in a bowl to blend.

Table-top Mixers

Table-top mixers are freestanding and are capable of dealing with fairly large quantities of mixture. They are robust machines and good for heavy cake mixing as well as whipping cream, whisking egg whites or making one-stage cakes. These mixers also offer a wide range of attachments ranging from liquidisers, mincers, juicers, can openers and many more and varied attachments.

Hand-held Mixers

Hand-held mixers are smaller than freestanding mixers and often come with their own bowl and stand from which they can be lifted off and used as hand-held devices. They have a motorised head with detachable twin whisks. These mixers are particularly versatile as they do not need a specific bowl in which to whisk. Any suitable mixing bowl can be used.

Essential Ingredients

The quantities may differ, but basic baking ingredients do not vary greatly. Let us take a closer look at the baking ingredients which are essential.

Fat

Butter and margarine are the fats most commonly used in baking. Others that can be used include white vegetable fat, lard and oil. Low-fat spreads are not recommended for baking, as they break down when cooked at a high temperature. Often it is a matter of personal preference which fat you choose but there are a few guidelines that are important to remember.

Butter and Margarine

Unsalted butter is the fat most commonly used in cake making, especially in rich fruit cakes and the heavier sponge cakes such as Madeira or chocolate torte. Unsalted butter gives a distinctive flavour to the cake. Some people favour margarine which imparts little or no flavour to the cake.

As a rule, butter and firm block margarine should not be used straight from the refrigerator but allowed to come to room temperature before using (allow about an hour to soften). Also, it should be beaten by itself first before creaming or rubbing in. Soft margarine is best suited to one-stage recipes.

Oil

Light oils, such as vegetable or sunflower, are sometimes used instead of solid fats. However, if oil is used, be careful – it is vital to follow a specific recipe because the proportions of oil to flour and eggs are different and these recipes will need extra raising agents.

Flour

We can buy a wide range of flour all designed for specific jobs. There is even a special sponge flour designed especially for whisked sponges. It is also possible to buy flours that cater for coeliacs, which contain no gluten. Buckwheat, soy and chickpea flours are also available. Flour can also come ready sifted.

Which Flour to Use

Strong flour, which is rich in gluten, whether it is white or brown (this includes granary and stoneground), is best kept for bread and Yorkshire pudding. Ordinary flour or weak flour is best for cakes, which absorb the fat easily and give a soft light texture. This flour comes in plain white or self-raising, as well as wholemeal. Self-raising flour, which has the raising agent already incorporated, is best kept for sponge cakes where it is important that an even rise is achieved.

Plain flour can be used for all types of baking. If using plain flour for cakes, unless otherwise stated in the recipe, use 1 teaspoon of baking powder to 225 g/8 oz of plain flour. With sponge cakes and light fruit cakes, it is best to use self-raising flour as the raising agent has already been added to the flour. This way there is no danger of using too much which can result in a sunken cake with a sour taste.

Other Raising Agents

There are other raising agents that are also used. Some cakes use bicarbonate of soda with or without cream of tartar, blended with warm or sour milk. Whisked eggs also act as a raising agent as the air trapped in the egg ensures that the mixture rises. Generally no other raising agent is required.

Eggs

There are many types of eggs sold and it really is a question of personal preference which ones are chosen. All offer the same nutritional benefits. Store eggs in the refrigerator with the round end uppermost and allow them to come to room temperature before using.

Sizes

When a recipe states 1 egg, it is generally accepted this refers to a medium egg. Over the past few years the grading of eggs has changed. For years, eggs were sold as small, standard and large, then this method changed and they were graded in numbers with 1 being the largest. The general feeling by the public was that this system was misleading, so now we buy our eggs as small, medium and large.

Types

The majority of eggs sold in this country come from caged hens. These are the cheapest eggs and the hens have been fed on a manufactured mixed diet. Barn eggs are from hens kept in barns who are free to roam within the barn. However, their diet is similar to caged hens and the barns may be overcrowded.

Free-range eggs are from hens that lead a much more natural life and are fed natural foods. This, however, is not always the case and in some instances they may still live in a crowded environment and fed the same foods as caged and barn hens. Organic eggs are from hens that live in a flock, whose beaks are not clipped and who are completely free to roam. Obviously, these eggs are much more expensive than the others.

Safety

Due to the slight risk of salmonella, all eggs are now sold date stamped to ensure that the eggs are used in their prime. This applies even to farm eggs which are no longer allowed to be sold straight from the farm. Look for the lion quality stamp (on 75 per cent of all eggs sold) which guarantees that the eggs come from hens vaccinated against salmonella, have been laid in the UK and are produced to the highest food safety and standards. All of these eggs carry a best-before date. Do remember that raw or semi-cooked eggs should not be given to babies, toddlers, pregnant women, the elderly and those suffering from a recurring illness.

Sugar

Sugar not only offers taste to baking but also adds texture and volume to the mixture.

Which Sugar to Use

It is generally accepted that caster sugar is best for sponge cakes. Its fine granules disperse evenly when creaming or whisking. Granulated sugar is used for more general cooking, such as stewing fruit, whereas demerara sugar with its toffee taste and crunchy texture is good for sticky puddings and cakes. For rich fruit cakes, Christmas puddings and cakes, use the muscovado sugars which give a rich intense treacle flavour. Icing sugar is used primarily for icings and can be used in fruit sauces when the sugar needs to dissolve quickly.

Flavoured Sugar

For a different taste try flavouring your own sugar. Place a vanilla pod in a screw-top jar, fill with caster sugar, screw down the lid and leave for 2–3 weeks before using. Top up after use or use thinly pared lemon or orange rind in the same manner.

Reducing Sugar Intake

If you are trying to reduce sugar intake then use the unrefined varieties, such as golden granulated, golden caster (pictured above left), demerara (above right) and the muscovado sugars. All of these are a little sweeter than their refined counterparts, so less is required. Alternatively, clear honey or fructose (fruit sugar) can reduce sugar intake as they have similar calories to sugar, but are twice as sweet.

Working with Chocolate

Chocolate can be used in cakes to create flavour and colour, as well as to decorate. Who can resist its charms?

Melting Chocolate

As a general rule, it is important not to allow any water to come into contact with the chocolate. In fact, a drop or two of water is more problematic than larger amounts, which may blend in. The melted chocolate will 'seize' (turn into a grainy, clumpy mess) and it will be impossible to bring it back to a smooth consistency.

Do not overheat chocolate or melt it by itself in a pan over a direct heat. Always use either a double boiler or a heatproof bowl set over a saucepan of water, but do not allow the bottom of the bowl to come into contact with the water. Check the chocolate every couple of minutes, reducing or extinguishing the heat under the saucepan, as necessary. Stir the chocolate once or twice during melting until it is smooth and no lumps remain. Do not cover the bowl once the chocolate has melted or condensation will form, water will drop into it and it will be ruined.

Microwaving is another way of melting chocolate, but again, caution is required. Follow the oven manufacturer's instructions together with the instructions on the chocolate and proceed with care. Melt the chocolate in bursts of 30–60 seconds, stirring well between bursts until the chocolate is smooth. If possible, stop microwaving before all the chocolate has melted and allow the residual heat in the chocolate to finish the job.

Making Chocolate Decorations

There are a few useful techniques for working with chocolate. None of them are very complicated, and all can be mastered easily with a little practice.

Curls
To make curls, melt the chocolate following your preferred method and then spread it in a thin layer over a cool surface, such as a marble slab, ceramic tile or piece of granite. Leave until just set but not hard. Take a clean paint scraper or cheese plane and set it at an angle to the surface of the chocolate, then push, taking a layer off the surface. This will curl until you release the pressure.

Caraque
Caraque are long thin curls. To make caraque, prepare the chocolate in the same way as for the curls. Use a large sharp knife and hold it at about a 45-degree angle to the chocolate. Hold the handle and the tip and scrape the knife towards you pulling the handle but keeping the tip more or less in the same place. This method makes thinner, tighter, longer curls.

Shaved and Grated Chocolate
Using a vegetable peeler, shave a thick block of chocolate to make mini-curls or use a sharp long-bladed knife to make big shavings. These are best achieved if the chocolate is a little soft, otherwise it has a tendency to break into little flakes. Or use a grater to achieve even tinier shavings.

Chocolate Shapes
Spread a thin layer of chocolate, as described in the instructions for chocolate curls, and allow to set as before. Use shaped cutters or a sharp knife to cut out shapes. Use to decorate your cakes.

Chocolate Modelling Paste
To make chocolate modelling paste (very useful for cake coverings and for making heavier shapes, like ribbons) put 200 g/7 oz plain chocolate in a bowl and add 3 tablespoons of liquid glucose. Set the bowl over a pan of gently simmering water. Stir until the chocolate is just melted then remove from the heat. Beat until smooth and leave the mixture to cool. When cool enough to handle, knead to a smooth paste on a clean work surface. The mixture can now be rolled and cut to shape. If the paste hardens, wrap it in clingfilm and warm it in the microwave for a few seconds on low.

Basic Methods

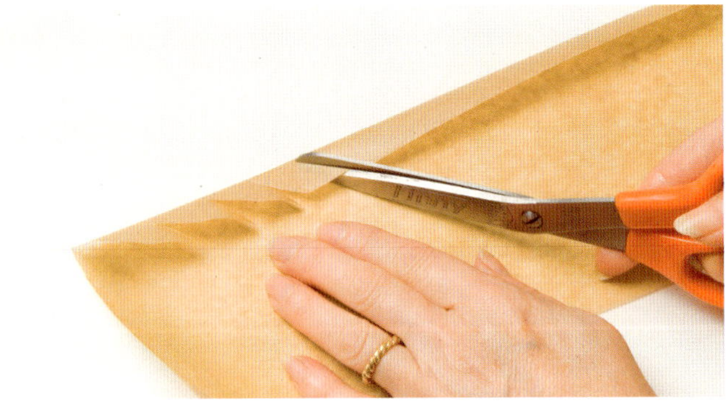

Lining

If a recipe states that the tin needs lining do not be tempted to ignore this. Rich fruit cakes and other cakes that take a long time to cook benefit from the tin being lined so that the edges and base do not burn or dry out.

Papers

Greaseproof paper or baking parchment is ideal for this. It is a good idea to have the paper at least double thickness, or preferably three to four layers. Sponge cakes and other cakes that are cooked in 30 minutes or less are also better if the bases are lined as it is far easier to remove them from the tin.

Technique

The best way to line a round or square tin is to draw lightly around the base and then cut just inside the markings making it easy to sit in the tin. Next, lightly oil the paper so it peels easily away from the cake. If the sides of the tin also need to be lined, then cut a strip of paper long enough for the tin. This can be measured by wrapping a piece of string around the rim of the tin. Once again, lightly oil the paper, push against the tin and oil once more as this will hold the paper to the sides of the tin.

Separating Eggs

When separating eggs (that is, separating the white from the yolk), crack an egg in half lightly and cleanly over a bowl, being careful not to break the yolk and keeping it in the shell. Then tip the yolk backwards and forwards between the two shell halves, allowing as much of the white as possible spill out into the bowl. Keep or discard the yolk and/or the white as needed. Make sure that you do not get any yolk in your whites as this will prevent successful whisking of the whites. It takes practice!

Different Mixing Techniques

Creaming

The creaming method – which means that the butter and sugar are first beaten or 'creamed' together – makes light cakes. A little care is needed for this method. Use a large

mixing bowl to beat the fat and sugar together until pale and fluffy. The eggs are gradually beaten in to form a slackened batter and the flour is folded in last, to stiffen up the mixture.

Rubbing In

In this method, the fat is lightly worked into the flour between the fingers, as in pastry-making, until the mixture resembles fine crumbs. This can be done by hand or in a food processor. Enough liquid is stirred in to give a soft mixture that will drop easily from a spoon. This method is used for easy fruit cakes.

All-In-One Mixtures

This 'one stage' method is quick and easy and is perfect for those new to baking, as it does not involve any complicated techniques. It is ideal for making light sponges, but soft tub-type margarine or softened butter at room temperature must be used. All the ingredients are simply placed in a large bowl and quickly beaten together for just a few minutes until smooth. Be careful not to overbeat, as this will make the mixture too wet. Self-raising flour with the addition of a little extra baking powder is vital for a good rise.

The Melting Method

Cakes with a delicious moist, sticky texture, such as gingerbread, are made by this method. These cakes use a high proportion of sugar and syrup, which are gently warmed together in a saucepan with the fat, until the sugar has dissolved and the mixture is liquid. It is important to cool the hot melted mixture a little before beating in flour, eggs and spices to make the batter, otherwise it will damage the power of the raising agent.

Icing Recipes

Cream Cheese Frosting

Covers a 20 cm/8 in round cake (top) or 12 cupcakes

50 g/2 oz unsalted butter, softened
300 g/11 oz icing sugar, sifted
flavouring of choice
food colourings
125 g/4 oz cream cheese

Beat the butter and icing sugar together until light and fluffy. Add the flavourings and colourings of choice and beat again. Add the cream cheese and whisk until light and fluffy. Do not overbeat, however, or the mixture can become runny.

Basic Buttercream

Covers a 20 cm/8 in round cake (top) or 12 cupcakes

150 g/5 oz unsalted butter, softened
225 g/8 oz icing sugar, sifted
2 tbsp hot milk or water
1 tsp vanilla extract
food colourings of choice

Beat the butter until light and fluffy, then beat in the sifted icing sugar and hot milk or water in two batches. Add the vanilla extract and any food colourings. Store chilled for up to 2 days in a lidded container.

Chocolate Fudge Frosting

Covers a 20 cm/8 in round cake (top) or 12 cupcakes

125 g/4 oz dark chocolate, broken into pieces
50 g/2 oz unsalted butter
1 medium egg, beaten
175 g/6 oz natural icing sugar, sifted
½ tsp vanilla extract

Place the chocolate and butter in a bowl over a pan of hot water and stir until melted. Remove from the heat and beat in the egg with the icing sugar and vanilla. Beat until smooth and glossy, then use immediately, or allow to cool and thicken for a spreading consistency.

Royal Icing

Covers a 20 cm/8 in round cake (top) or 12 cupcakes

2 medium egg whites
500 g/1 lb 2 oz icing sugar, sifted
2 tsp lemon juice

Put the egg whites in a large bowl and whisk lightly with a fork to break up the whites until foamy. Sift in half the icing sugar with the lemon juice and beat well with an electric mixer for 4 minutes or by hand with a wooden spoon for about 10 minutes until smooth.

Gradually sift in the remaining icing sugar and beat again until thick, smooth and brilliant white and the icing forms soft peaks when flicked up with a spoon. Keep the royal icing covered with a clean damp cloth until you are ready to use it, or store in the refrigerator in a tightly lidded plastic container until needed. If making royal icing ahead of time to use later, beat it again before use to remove any air bubbles that may have formed in the mixture.

Glacé Icing

Covers a 20 cm/8 in round cake (top) or 12 cupcakes

225 g/8 oz icing sugar
few drops lemon juice, or vanilla or almond extract
2–3 tbsp boiling water
liquid food colouring

Sift the confectioners' sugar into a bowl and add the chosen flavouring. Gradually stir in enough water to mix to a consistency of thick cream. Beat with a wooden spoon until the icing is thick enough to coat the back of the spoon. Add colouring, if liked, and use at once because the icing will begin to form a skin.

Apricot Glaze

Covers two 20 cm/8 in round cakes (top) or 24 cupcakes

450 g/1 lb apricot jam
3 tbsp water
1 tsp lemon juice

Place the jam, water and juice in a heavy-based saucepan and heat gently, stirring, until soft and melted. Boil rapidly for 1 minute, then press through a fine sieve with the back of a

wooden spoon. Discard the pieces of fruit. Use immediately for glazing or sticking on almond paste and/or fondant, or pour into a clean jar or plastic container, seal and refrigerate for up to 3 months.

Almond Paste

Covers two 20 cm/8 in round cakes (top) or 24 cupcakes

125 g/4 oz icing sugar, sifted
125 g/4 oz caster sugar
225 g/8 oz ground almonds
1 medium egg
1 tsp lemon juice

Stir the sugars and ground almonds together in a bowl. Whisk the egg and lemon juice together and mix into the dry ingredients.

Knead until the paste is smooth. Wrap tightly in clingfilm or foil to keep airtight and store in the refrigerator until needed. The paste can be made 2–3 days ahead of time, but, after that, it will start to dry out and become difficult to handle.

To use the almond paste, knead on a surface lightly dusted with icing sugar until soft and pliable. Brush the top of each cake with apricot glaze. Roll out the paste and cut out discs large enough to cover the tops of the cakes. Press onto the cakes.

Rolling Fondant (Also known as 'sugarpaste')

Covers a 20 cm/8 in round cake (top) or 12 cupcakes, or use for decorations

1 medium egg white
1 tbsp liquid glucose
350 g/12 oz icing sugar, sifted

Place the egg white and liquid glucose in a large mixing bowl and stir together with a fork, breaking up the egg white. Add the icing sugar gradually, mixing in with a palette knife until the mixture binds together and forms a ball. Turn the ball of fondant out onto a clean surface dusted with icing sugar and knead for 5 minutes until soft but firm enough to roll out. If the icing is too soft, knead in a little more icing sugar until the mixture is pliable.

To colour, knead in paste food colouring. Do not use liquid food colouring because this is not suitable and will make the fondant go limp.

To use, roll out thinly on a clean surface dusted with icing sugar and cut out a disc large enough to cover the top of each cake. Brush the almond paste (if using as a layer under the fondant) with a little cold boiled water or a clear spirit, such as kirsch, then press onto the cake and press the fondant disc on top of the almond paste. Or coat the cakes with a little buttercream and press down the fondant disc on top.

To mould, knead lightly and roll out thinly on a surface dusted with icing sugar. Use cutters or templates to make flat shapes, then mould into three-dimensional shapes with your fingertips and leave to dry for 24 hours in egg cartons lined with clingfilm.

Special Occasion & Dessert Cakes

Sauternes & Olive Oil Cake

Cuts into 8–10 slices

125 g/4 oz plain flour, plus extra for dusting
4 medium eggs
125 g/4 oz caster sugar
grated zest of ½ lemon
grated zest of ½ orange
2 tbsp Sauternes or other sweet dessert wine
3 tbsp very best quality extra-virgin olive oil
4 ripe peaches
1–2 tsp soft brown sugar, or to taste
1 tbsp lemon juice
icing sugar, to dust

1. Preheat oven to 140°C/275°F/Gas Mark 1. Oil and line a 25.5 cm/10 inch springform tin. Sift the flour onto a large sheet of greaseproof paper and reserve. Using a freestanding electric mixer, if possible, whisk the eggs and sugar together, until pale and stiff. Add the lemon and orange zest.

2. Turn the speed to low and pour the flour from the paper in a slow, steady stream onto the eggs and sugar mixture. Add the wine and olive oil and switch the machine off as the olive oil should not be incorporated completely.

3. Fold the mixture very gently three or four times so that the ingredients are just incorporated. Pour the mixture immediately into the tin and bake in the oven for 20–25 minutes, without opening the door for at least 15 minutes. Test if cooked by pressing the top lightly with a clean finger – if it springs back, remove from the oven, if not, bake for a little longer.

4. Leave the cake to cool in the tin on a wire rack. Remove from the tin when cool enough to handle. Skin the peaches and cut into segments. Toss with the brown sugar and lemon juice and reserve. When the cake is cold, dust with icing sugar, cut into wedges and serve with the peaches.

Peach & White Chocolate Gateau

Cuts into 8–10 slices

175 g/6 oz unsalted butter, softened
2 tsp grated orange zest
175 g/6 oz caster sugar
3 medium eggs
100 g/3½ oz white chocolate, melted and cooled
225 g/8 oz self-raising flour, sifted

For the filling and topping:

2 ripe peaches, peeled and chopped
2 tbsp peach or orange liqueur
600 ml/1 pint double cream
75 g/3 oz icing sugar
125 g/4 oz hazelnuts, toasted and chopped

1. Preheat the oven to 170°C/325°F/Gas Mark 3, 10 minutes before baking. Lightly oil and line a deep 23 cm/9 inch round cake tin. Cream the butter, orange zest and sugar together until light and fluffy. Add the eggs, 1 at a time, beating after each addition, then beat in the chocolate.

2. Add the flour and 175 ml/6 fl oz of water in two batches. Spoon into the prepared tin and bake in the oven for 1½ hours or until firm. Leave to stand for at least 5 minutes before turning out onto a wire rack to cool completely.

3. For the filling, place the peaches in a bowl and pour over the liqueur. Leave to stand for 30 minutes. Whip half the cream with half the icing sugar until soft peaks form, then fold in the peach mixture.

4. Split the cold cake in to three layers, place one layer on a plate and spread with half the filling. Top with a second sponge layer and spread with the remaining filling. Top with the last layer. Whip the remaining cream and icing sugar together until soft peaks form. Spread over the top and sides of the cake. Press the hazelnuts into the side of cake. Chill in the refrigerator until required. Serve cut into slices. Store in the refrigerator.

Supreme Chocolate Gateau

Cuts into 10–12 slices

175 g/6 oz self-raising flour, sifted
1½ tsp baking powder, sifted
3 tbsp cocoa powder, sifted
175 g/6 oz margarine or butter, softened
175 g/6 oz caster sugar
3 large eggs

To decorate:
350 g/12 oz dark chocolate
1 gelatine leaf
200 ml/7 fl oz double cream
75 g/3 oz butter
cocoa powder for dusting

1. Preheat the oven to 180°C/350°F/Gas Mark 4, 10 minutes before baking. Lightly oil and line three 20.5 cm/8 inch round cake tins.

2. Place all the cake ingredients into a bowl and whisk together until thick. Add a little warm water if very thick. Divide the mixture evenly between the prepared tins. Bake in the preheated oven for 35–40 minutes until a skewer inserted in the centre comes out clean. Cool on wire racks.

3. Very gently heat 2 tablespoons hot water with 50 g/2 oz of the chocolate and stir until combined. Remove from the heat and leave for 5 minutes.

4. Place the gelatine into a shallow dish and add 2 tablespoons cold water. Leave for 5 minutes then squeeze out any excess water and add to the chocolate and water mixture. Stir until dissolved.

5. Whip the double cream until just thickened. Add the chocolate mixture and continue whisking until soft peaks form. Leave until starting to set.

6. Place one of the cakes onto a plate and spread with half the cream mixture. Top with a second cake and the rest of the cream, cover with the third cake and chill in the refrigerator until the cream has set.

7. Melt 175 g/6 oz of the chocolate with the butter and stir until smooth. Leave until thickened.

8. Melt the remaining chocolate. Cut out twelve 10 cm/4 inch squares of foil. Spread the chocolate evenly over the squares to within 2.5 cm/1 inch of the edges. Refrigerate for 3–4 minutes until just set but not brittle. Gather up the corners and crimp together. Return to the refrigerator until firm.

9. Spread the chocolate and butter mixture over the top and sides of the cake. Remove the foil from the giant curls and use to decorate the top of the cake. Dust with cocoa powder and serve cut into wedges.

White Chocolate & Raspberry Mousse Gateau

Cuts into 8 slices

4 medium eggs
125 g/4 oz caster sugar
75 g/3 oz plain flour, sifted
25 g/1 oz cornflour, sifted
3 gelatine leaves
450 g/1 lb raspberries, thawed if frozen
400 g/14 oz white chocolate
200 g/7 oz plain fromage frais
2 medium egg whites
25 g/1 oz caster sugar
4 tbsp raspberry or orange liqueur
200 ml/7 fl oz double cream
fresh raspberries, halved, to decorate

1. Preheat the oven to 190°C/375°F/Gas Mark 5, 10 minutes before baking. Oil and line two 23 cm/9 inch cake tins. Whisk the eggs and sugar until thick and creamy and the whisk leaves a trail. Fold in the flour and cornflour. Divide between the tins. Bake in the oven for 12–15 minutes until risen and firm. Cool in the tins, turn out onto wire racks.

2. Place the gelatine with 4 tablespoons of cold water in a dish and leave to soften for 5 minutes. Purée half the raspberries, press through a sieve, then heat until nearly boiling. Squeeze out excess water from the gelatine, add to the purée and stir until dissolved. Reserve.

3. Melt 175 g/6 oz of the chocolate in a bowl over a saucepan of simmering water. Leave to cool, then stir in the fromage frais and purée. Whisk the egg whites until stiff and whisk in the sugar. Fold into the raspberry mixture with the rest of the raspberries.

4. Line the sides of a 23 cm/9 inch springform tin with nonstick baking parchment. Place one layer of sponge in the base and sprinkle with half the liqueur. Pour in the raspberry mixture and top with the second sponge. Brush with the remaining liqueur. Press down and chill in the refrigerator for 4 hours. Unmould onto a plate.

5. Cut a strip of double thickness nonstick baking parchment to fit around the cake and stand 1 cm/½ inch higher. Melt the remaining white chocolate and spread thickly onto the parchment. Leave until just setting. Wrap around the cake and freeze for 15 minutes. Peel away the parchment. Whip the cream until thick and spread over the top. Decorate with raspberries.

Pink Candle Cupcakes

Makes 12

75 g/3 oz fresh raspberries
150 g/5 oz butter, softened
150 g/5 oz caster sugar
175 g/6 oz self-raising flour
3 medium eggs
1 tsp vanilla extract

To decorate:
1 batch cream cheese frosting (*see* page 23)
pink liquid food colouring
small pink candles

1. Preheat the oven to 180°C/350°F/Gas Mark 4. Line a 12-hole muffin tray with deep paper cases.

2. Press the raspberries through the sieve to make a purée. Cream the butter and sugar in a bowl, then sift in the flour. In another bowl, beat the eggs with the vanilla extract, then add to the butter and sugar mixture. Beat until smooth, then fold in the purée. Spoon into the cases, filling them three-quarters full.

3. Bake for about 18 minutes until firm to the touch in the centre. Turn out to cool on a wire rack.

4. Colour the frosting pink with a few dots of food colouring. Place in a piping bag fitted with a star nozzle and pipe large swirls on top of each cupcake. Top each cupcake with a tiny candle. Keep for 3 days in an airtight container in a cool place.

Celebration Fruit Cake

Cuts into 16 slices

125 g/4 oz butter or margarine
125 g/4 oz soft dark brown sugar
400-g can crushed pineapple
150 g/5 oz raisins
150 g/5 oz sultanas
125 g/4 oz crystallised ginger, finely chopped
125 g/4 oz glacé cherries, coarsely chopped
125 g/4 oz mixed cut peel
225 g/8 oz self-raising flour
1 tsp bicarbonate of soda
2 tsp mixed spice
1 tsp ground cinnamon
½ tsp salt
2 large eggs, beaten

For the topping:
100 g/3½ oz pecan or walnut halves, lightly toasted
125 g/4 oz red, green and yellow glacé cherries
100 g/3½ oz small pitted prunes or dates
2 tbsp clear honey

1. Preheat the oven to 170°C/325°F/Gas Mark 3, 10 minutes before baking. Heat the butter and sugar in a saucepan until the sugar has dissolved. Stir frequently.

2. Add the pineapple and juice, dried fruits and peel. Bring to the boil, simmer for 3 minutes, stirring occasionally. Remove from the heato to cool completely.

3. Lightly oil and line the base of a 20.5 x 7.5 cm/8 x 3 inch loose-bottomed cake tin with nonstick baking parchment. Sift the flour, bicarbonate of soda, spices and salt into a bowl.

4. Add the boiled fruit mixture to the flour with the eggs and mix. Spoon into the tin and smooth the top. Bake in the oven for 1¼ hours, or until a skewer inserted into the centre comes out clean. (If browning too quickly, cover loosely with foil and reduce the oven temperature.) Cool completely before removing from the tin and discarding the paper.

5. Arrange the nuts, cherries and prunes or dates in a pattern on top of the cake. Heat the honey and brush over the topping to glaze. Alternatively, toss the nuts and fruits in the warm honey and spread evenly over the top of the cake. Cool completely and store in a cake tin for a day or two before serving to allow the flavours to develop.

Marzipan Cake

Cuts into 12–14 slices

450 g/1 lb blanched almonds
300 g/11 oz icing sugar (includes sugar for dusting and rolling)
4 medium egg whites
125 g/4 oz Madeira cake
2 tbsp Marsala wine
225 g/8 oz ricotta cheese
50 g/2 oz caster sugar
grated zest of 1 lemon
50 g/2 oz candied peel, finely chopped
25 g/1 oz glacé cherries, finely chopped
425-g can peach halves, drained
200 ml/⅓ pint double cream

1. Grind the almonds in a food processor until fairly fine. Mix with 200 g/7 oz of icing sugar. Beat the egg whites until stiff, fold into the almond mixture to form a stiffish dough. It will be quite sticky but firm up as it rests. Leave for 30 minutes.

2. Dust a work surface with some of the remaining icing sugar so that the marzipan does not stick. Roll out two thirds of the marzipan into a large sheet to a thickness of about 5 mm/¼ inch. Use to line a sloping-sided baking dish with a base measuring 25.5 cm x 20.5 cm/10 x 8 inches. Trim the edges and put any trimmings with the rest of the marzipan.

3. Cut the cake into thin slices and make a layer of sponge to cover the bottom of the marzipan. Sprinkle with the wine. Beat the ricotta with the sugar and add the lemon zest, candied peel and cherries. Spread this over the sponge. Slice the peaches, put them on top of the ricotta. Whip the cream and spread it over the peaches. Roll out the remaining marzipan and lay it over the cream to seal the whole cake, pressing down gently to remove any air. Press the edges of the marzipan together. Chill in the refrigerator for 2 hours. Turn the cake out on to a serving plate and dust generously with icing sugar. Slice thickly and serve immediately.

Christmas Cranberry Chocolate Roulade

Cuts into 12–14 slices

5 large eggs, separated
3 tbsp cocoa powder, sifted, plus extra for dusting
125 g/4 oz icing sugar, sifted, plus extra for dusting
¼ tsp cream of tartar

For the frosting:
300 ml/½ pint double cream
350 g/12 oz dark chocolate, chopped
2 tbsp brandy (optional)

For the filling:
175 g/6 oz cranberry sauce
1–2 tbsp brandy (optional)
450 ml/¾ pint double cream, whipped to soft peaks

To decorate:
caramelised orange strips
dried cranberries

1. Make the frosting first. Bring the cream to the boil over a medium heat. Remove and add all of the chocolate, stirring until melted. Stir in the brandy, if using and strain into a bowl. Cool, then refrigerate for 6–8 hours.

2. Preheat the oven to 200°C/400°F/Gas Mark 6. Lightly oil and line a 39 x 26 cm/15½ x 10½ inch Swiss roll tin with nonstick baking parchment. Using an electric mixer, beat the egg yolks until thick and creamy. Slowly beat in the cocoa powder and half the icing sugar and reserve.

3. Whisk the egg whites and cream of tartar into soft peaks. Gradually whisk in the remaining sugar until the mixture is stiff and glossy. Gently fold the yolk mixture into the egg whites. Spread evenly into the tin. Bake in the oven for 15 minutes.

4. Remove and invert on to greaseproof paper dusted with cocoa powder. Cut off the crisp edges of the cake then roll up. Leave on a wire rack until cold.

5. For the filling, heat the cranberry sauce with the brandy until warm and spreadable. Unroll the cake and spread with the cranberry sauce. Allow to cool and set. Spoon the whipped cream over the surface and spread to within 2.5 cm/1 inch of the edges. Re-roll the cake. Transfer to a cake plate or tray.

6. Allow the chocolate ganache to soften at room temperature, then beat until soft and of a spreadable consistency. Spread over the roulade and, using a fork, mark the roulade with ridges. Dust with icing sugar. Decorate with the orange strips and dried cranberries and serve.

Wild Strawberry & Rose Petal Jam Cake

Cuts into 8 slices

275 g/10 oz plain flour
1 tsp baking powder
¼ tsp salt
150 g/5 oz unsalted butter, softened
200 g/7 oz caster sugar
2 large eggs, beaten
2 tbsp rosewater
125 ml/4 fl oz milk
frosted rose petals, to decorate

For the rose cream filling:
200 ml/7 fl oz double cream
25 ml/1 fl oz natural Greek yogurt
2 tbsp rosewater
1–2 tbsp icing sugar
125 g/4 oz strawberry or rose petal jam, slightly warmed
125 g/4 oz wild strawberries, hulled, or baby strawberries, chopped

1. Preheat the oven to 180°C/350°F/Gas Mark 4, 10 minutes before baking. Lightly oil and flour a 20.5 cm/8 inch nonstick cake tin. Sift the flour, baking powder and salt into a bowl and reserve.

2. Beat the butter and sugar until light and fluffy. Beat in the eggs, a little at a time, then stir in the rosewater. Gently fold in the flour mixture and milk and mix lightly together. Spoon into the tin, spreading evenly and smoothing the top.

3. Bake in the oven for 25–30 minutes, or until well risen and golden and the centre springs back when pressed with a clean finger. Remove and cool, then remove from the tin.

4. For the filling, whisk the cream, yogurt, half the rosewater and 1 tablespoon of icing sugar until soft peaks form. Split the cake horizontally in half and sprinkle with the remaining rosewater. Spread the warmed jam on the base of the cake. Top with half the whipped cream mixture, then sprinkle with half the strawberries. Place the other cake half on top. Spread with the remaining cream. Decorate with the rose petals. Dust the cake with a little icing sugar and serve.

Black Forest Gateau

Cuts into 10–12 slices

250 g/9 oz butter
1 tbsp instant coffee granules
350 ml/12 fl oz hot water
200 g/7 oz dark chocolate, chopped or broken
400 g/14 oz caster sugar
225 g/8 oz self-raising flour
150 g/5 oz plain flour
50 g/2 oz cocoa powder
2 medium eggs
2 tsp vanilla extract
2 x 400-g cans stoned cherries in juice
2 tsp arrowroot
600 ml/1 pint double cream
50 ml/2 fl oz kirsch

1. Preheat the oven to 150°C/300°F/Gas Mark 2, 5 minutes before serving. Lightly oil and line a deep 23 cm/9 inch cake tin. Melt the butter in a large saucepan.

2. Blend the coffee with the hot water, add to the butter with the chocolate and sugar and heat gently, stirring until smooth. Pour into a large bowl and leave until just warm.

3. Sift together the flours and cocoa powder. Using an electric mixer, whisk the warm chocolate mixture on a low speed, then gradually whisk in the dry ingredients. Whisk in the eggs 1 at a time, then the vanilla extract.

4. Pour the mixture into the prepared tin and bake in the preheated oven for 1 hour 45 minutes or until firm and a skewer inserted into the centre comes out clean. Leave in the tin for 5 minutes to cool slightly before turning out onto a wire rack.

5. Place the cherries and their juice in a small saucepan and heat gently. Blend the arrowroot with 2 teaspoons of water until smooth, then stir into the cherries. Cook, stirring, until the liquid thickens. Simmer very gently for 2 minutes, then leave until cold.

6. Whisk the double cream until thick. Trim the top of the cake if necessary, then split the cake into three layers.

7. Brush the base of the cake with half the kirsch. Top with a layer of cream and one-third of the cherries. Repeat the layering, then place the third layer on top.

8. Reserve a little cream for decorating and use the remainder to cover the top and sides of the cake. Pipe a decorative edge around the cake, then arrange the remaining cherries in the centre and serve.

Chocolate Holly Leaf Cupcakes

Makes 12

125 g/4 oz caster sugar
125 g/4 oz soft tub margarine
2 medium eggs
125 g/4 oz self-raising flour
½ tsp baking powder
50 g/2 oz dark or milk chocolate chips

To decorate:
12 holly leaves, washed and dried
75 g/3 oz dark chocolate, melted
50 g/2 oz unsalted butter, softened
300 g/11 oz icing sugar, sifted
125 g/4 oz full-fat cream cheese
50 g/2 oz milk chocolate, melted and cooled
1 tsp vanilla extract

1. Preheat the oven to 190°C/375°F/Gas Mark 5. Line a 12-hole muffin tray with deep paper cases.

2. Place all the cupcake ingredients except the chocolate chips in a large bowl and beat with an electric mixer for about 2 minutes until smooth. Fold in the chocolate chips, then fill the paper cases halfway up with the mixture. Bake for about 15 minutes until firm, risen and golden. Remove to a wire rack to cool.

3. To decorate the cupcakes, paint the underside of each holly leaf with the melted dark chocolate. Leave to dry out on nonstick baking parchment for 1 hour, or in the refrigerator for 30 minutes.

4. Beat the butter until soft, then gradually beat in the icing sugar until light. Add the cream cheese and whisk until fluffy. Divide the mixture in half and beat the cooled melted milk chocolate into one half and the vanilla extract into the other half. Fit a piping bag with a wide star nozzle and spoon chocolate icing on one side of the bag and the vanilla icing on the other. Pipe swirls on top of the cupcakes.

5. Peel the holly leaves away from the set chocolate and decorate the top of each cupcake with a chocolate leaf. Keep for 3 days in an airtight container in a cool place.

Coffee & Walnut Gateau with Brandied Prunes

Cuts into 10–12 slices

450 g/1 lb walnut pieces
50 g/2 oz self-raising flour
½ tsp baking powder
1 tsp instant coffee powder (not granules)
5 large eggs, separated
¼ tsp cream of tartar
150 g/5 oz caster sugar
2 tbsp sunflower oil
8 walnut halves, to decorate

For the prunes:

225 g/8 oz ready-to-eat pitted dried prunes
150 ml/¼ pint cold tea
3 tbsp brandy

For the filling:

600 ml/1 pint double cream
4 tbsp icing sugar, sifted
2 tbsp coffee-flavoured liqueur

1. Preheat the oven to 180°C/350°F/Gas Mark 4, 10 minutes before baking. Put the prunes in a bowl with the tea and brandy and allow to stand for at least 3–4 hours. Oil and line the bases of two 23 cm/9 inch cake tins.

2. Chop the walnut pieces in a food processor. Reserve a quarter of the nuts. Add the flour, baking powder and coffee and blend until finely ground.

3. Whisk the egg whites with the cream of tartar until soft peaks form. Sprinkle in a third of the sugar, 2 tablespoons at a time, until stiff peaks form.

4. In another bowl, beat the egg yolks, oil and remaining sugar, until thick. Alternately fold in the nut mixture and egg whites until just blended.

5. Divide the mixture between the tins, smoothing the tops. Bake in the oven for 30–35 minutes, or until the top of the cakes spring back when lightly pressed with a finger. Remove and cool. Remove from the tins and discard the paper.

6. Drain the prunes, reserving the soaking liquid. Dry on kitchen paper, then chop and reserve.

7. Whisk the cream with the icing sugar and liqueur until soft peaks form. Spoon one-eighth of the cream into a pastry bag with a star nozzle.

8. Cut the cake layers in half horizontally. Sprinkle each cut side with 1 tablespoon of the reserved prune-soaking liquid. Sandwich the cakes together with half of the cream and all of the chopped prunes.

9. Spread the remaining cream around the sides of the cake and press in the reserved chopped walnuts. Pipe rosettes around the edge of the cake. Decorate with walnut halves and serve.

Orange Fruit Cake

Cuts into 10–12 slices

225 g/8 oz self-raising flour
2 tsp baking powder
225 g/8 oz caster sugar
225 g/8 oz butter, softened
4 large eggs
grated zest of 1 orange
2 tbsp orange juice
2–3 tbsp Cointreau
125 g/4 oz chopped nuts
Cape gooseberries, blueberries, raspberries and mint sprigs to decorate
icing sugar, to dust (optional)

For the filling:
450 ml/¾ pint double cream
50 ml/2 fl oz Greek yogurt
½ tsp vanilla extract
2–3 tbsp Cointreau
1 tbsp icing sugar
450 g/1 lb orange fruits, such as mango, peach, nectarine, papaya and yellow plums

1. Preheat the oven to 180°C/350°F/Gas Mark 4, 10 minutes before baking. Lightly oil and line the base of a 25.5 cm/10 inch deep cake tin or springform tin with nonstick baking parchment.

2. Sift the flour and baking powder into a large bowl and stir in the sugar. Make a well in the centre and add the butter, eggs, grated zest and orange juice. Beat until blended and a smooth batter is formed. Turn into the tin and smooth the top. Bake in the oven for 35–45 minutes, or until golden and the sides begin to shrink from the edge of the tin. Remove, cool before removing from the tin and discard the lining paper. Using a serrated knife, slice off the top third of the cake, cutting horizontally. Sprinkle the cut sides with the Cointreau.

3. For the filling, whip the cream and yogurt with the vanilla extract, Cointreau and icing sugar until soft peaks form. Chop the orange fruit and fold into the cream. Spread some of this mixture on to the bottom cake layer. Transfer to a serving plate.

4. Cover with the top layer of sponge and spread the remaining cream mixture over the top and sides. Press the chopped nuts into the sides and decorate the top with the Cape gooseberries, blueberries and raspberries. If liked, dust with icing sugar. Serve.

Almond Angel Cake with Amaretto Cream

Cuts into 10–12 slices

175 g/6 oz icing sugar, plus 2–3 tbsp
150 g/5 oz plain flour
350 ml/12 fl oz egg whites (about 10 large egg whites)
1½ tsp cream of tartar
½ tsp vanilla extract
1 tsp almond extract
¼ tsp salt
200 g/7 oz caster sugar
175 ml/6 fl oz double cream
2 tablespoons Amaretto liqueur
fresh raspberries, to decorate

1. Preheat the oven to 180°C/350°F/Gas Mark 4, 10 minutes before baking. Sift together the 175 g/6 oz icing sugar and flour. Stir to blend, then sift again and reserve.

2. Using an electric mixer, beat the egg whites, cream of tartar, vanilla extract, ½ teaspoon of almond extract and salt on medium speed until soft peaks form. Gradually add the caster sugar, 2 tablespoons at a time, beating well after each addition, until stiff peaks form.

3. Sift about one third of the flour mixture over the egg white mixture and using a metal spoon or rubber spatula, gently fold into the egg white mixture.

4. Repeat, folding the flour mixture into the egg white mixture in two more batches. Spoon gently into an ungreased angel food cake tin or 25.5 cm/10 inch tube tin.

5. Bake in the preheated oven until risen and golden on top and the surface springs back quickly when gently pressed with a clean finger. Immediately invert the cake tin and cool completely in the tin.

6. When cool, carefully run a sharp knife around the edge of the tin and the centre ring to loosen the cake from the edge. Using the fingertips, ease the cake from the tin and invert onto a cake plate. Thickly dust the cake with the extra icing sugar.

7. Whip the cream with the remaining almond extract, Amaretto liqueur and a little more icing sugar, until soft peaks form.

8. Fill a piping bag fitted with a star nozzle with half the cream and pipe around the bottom edge of the cake. Decorate the edge with the fresh raspberries and serve the remaining cream separately.

Black & White Torte

Cuts into 8–10 slices

4 medium eggs
150 g/5 oz caster sugar
50 g/2 oz cornflour
50 g/2 oz plain flour
50 g/2 oz self-raising flour
900 ml/1½ pints double cream
150 g/5 oz dark chocolate, chopped
300 g/11 oz white chocolate, chopped
6 tbsp Grand Marnier, or other orange liqueur
cocoa powder for dusting

1. Preheat the oven to 180°C/350°F/Gas Mark 4, 10 minutes before baking. Lightly oil and line a 23 cm/9 inch round cake tin. Beat the eggs and sugar in a large bowl until thick and creamy. Sift together the cornflour, plain flour and self-raising flour three times, then lightly fold into the egg mixture. Spoon the mixture into the prepared tin and bake in the preheated oven for 35–40 minutes or until firm. Turn the cake out onto a wire rack and leave to cool.

2. Place 300 ml/½ pint of the cream in a saucepan and bring to the boil. Remove from the heat, add the dark chocolate and a tablespoon of the liqueur. Stir until smooth. Repeat using the remaining cream, white chocolate and 2 tablespoons of the liqueur. Refrigerate for 2 hours, then whisk each mixture until thick and creamy. Place the dark chocolate mixture in a piping bag with a plain nozzle and half the white chocolate mixture in a separate piping bag with a plain nozzle. Reserve the remaining white chocolate mixture.

3. Split the cold cake horizontally into two layers. Brush or drizzle the remaining 3 tablespoons of liqueur over the cakes. Put one layer onto a serving plate. Pipe alternating rings of white and dark chocolate mixture to cover the first layer of cake. Use the reserved white chocolate mixture to cover the top and sides of the cake. Dust with cocoa powder, cut into slices and serve. Store in the refrigerator.

Sachertorte

Cuts into 10–12 slices

150 g/5 oz dark chocolate
150 g/5 oz unsalted butter, softened
125 g/4 oz caster sugar, plus 2 tbsp
3 medium eggs, separated
150 g/5 oz plain flour, sifted

To decorate:
225 g/8 oz apricot jam
125 g/4 oz dark chocolate, chopped
125 g/4 oz unsalted butter
25 g/1 oz milk chocolate

1. Preheat the oven to 180°C/350°F/Gas Mark 4, 10 minutes before baking. Lightly oil and line a deep 23 cm/9 inch cake tin.

2. Melt the 150 g/5 oz of chocolate in a heatproof bowl set over a saucepan of simmering water. Stir in 1 tablespoon water and leave to cool. Beat the butter and 125 g/4 oz of the sugar together until light and fluffy. Beat in the egg yolks, one at a time, beating well between each addition. Stir in the melted chocolate, then the flour.

3. In a clean grease-free bowl, whisk the egg whites until stiff peaks form, then whisk in the remaining sugar. Fold into the chocolate mixture and spoon into the tin. Bake in the oven for 30 minutes until firm. Leave for 5 minutes, then turn out onto a wire rack to cool. Leave upside down.

4. To decorate, split in two, place half on a plate. Heat the jam and rub through a fine sieve. Brush half the jam onto the first cake half, then cover with the other cake layer. Brush with the remaining jam. Leave for 1 hour or until the jam has set. Place the dark chocolate with the butter into a heatproof bowl over a saucepan of simmering water until melted. Stir occasionally until smooth, leave until thickened. Cover the cake. Melt the milk chocolate in a heatproof bowl over a saucepan of simmering water. Place in a small greaseproof piping bag and snip a small hole at the tip. Pipe Sacher with a large 'S' on the top. Leave to set at room temperature.

acher

Christmas Cake

Cuts into 12–14 slices

900 g/2 lb mixed dried fruit
75 g/3 oz glacé cherries, rinsed and halved
3 tbsp brandy or orange juice
finely grated zest and juice of 1 lemon
225 g/8 oz soft dark muscovado sugar
225 g/8 oz butter, at room temperature
4 medium eggs, beaten
225 g/8 oz plain flour
1 tbsp black treacle
1 tbsp mixed spice

To decorate:
2–4 tbsp brandy (optional)
4 tbsp sieved apricot jam
700 g/1½ lb almond paste
1 kg/ 2 lb 3 oz ready-to-roll sugarpaste
icing sugar, for dusting
decorations and ribbon

1. Place the mixed dried fruit and cherries in a bowl and sprinkle over the brandy or orange juice and the lemon zest and juice. Stir and leave to soak for 2–4 hours.

2. Preheat the oven to 150°C/300°F/Gas Mark 2. Grease and double line the base and sides of a 20.5 cm/8 inch round deep cake tin. Beat the sugar and butter together until soft and fluffy. Beat the eggs in gradually, adding 1 teaspoon flour with each addition. Stir in the treacle, sift in the rest of the flour and the spice. Add the soaked fruit and stir until the mixture is smooth.

3. Spoon into the tin, smooth the top level. Bake for 1 hour, then reduce the temperature to 140°C/275°F/Gas Mark 1 and bake for a further 2–2½ hours until a skewer inserted into the centre comes out clean. Leave to cool in the tin, then, when completely cold, remove, wrap in greaseproof paper and then in foil. Store in a cool place for 1–3 months.

4. To decorate, brush the cake all over with brandy, if using. Heat the jam and brush over the top and sides. Roll out one third of the almond paste and cut into a disc the size of the top of the cake using the empty tin as a guide. Place the disc on top. Roll the remaining paste into a strip long enough to cover the sides of the cake and press on. Leave the almond paste to dry out for 2 days in a cool place.

5. On a surface dusted with icing sugar, roll out the sugarpaste to a circle large enough to cover the top and sides of the cake. Brush 1 tablespoon brandy, or cold boiled water, over the almond paste and place the sugarpaste on top. Smooth down and trim. Make a border from tiny balls of sugarpaste and decorate.

Apple & Cinnamon Crisp-Top Cake

Cuts into 8 slices

For the topping:
350 g/12 oz eating apples, peeled
1 tbsp lemon juice
125 g/4 oz self-raising flour
1 tsp ground cinnamon
75 g/3 oz butter or margarine
75 g/3 oz demerara sugar
1 tbsp milk

For the base:
125 g/4 oz butter or margarine
125 g/4 oz caster sugar
2 medium eggs
150 g/5 oz self-raising flour
cream or freshly made custard, to serve

1. Preheat the oven to 180°C/350°F/Gas Mark 4, 10 minutes before baking. Lightly oil and line the base of a 20.5 cm/ 8 inch deep round cake tin with greaseproof paper or baking parchment.

2. Finely chop the apples and mix with the lemon juice. Reserve while making the cake.

3. For the crumble topping, sift the flour and cinnamon together into a large bowl. Rub the butter or margarine into the flour and cinnamon until the mixture resembles coarse breadcrumbs. Stir in the sugar and reserve.

4. For the base, cream the butter or margarine and sugar together until light and fluffy. Gradually beat the eggs into the sugar and butter mixture a little at a time until all the egg has been added. Sift the flour and gently fold in with a metal spoon or rubber spatula.

5. Spoon into the base of the prepared cake tin. Arrange the apple pieces on top, then lightly stir the milk into the crumble mixture. Scatter the crumble mixture over the apples and bake in the preheated oven for 1 ½ hours. Serve cold with cream or custard.

Chocolate Cakes

Double Chocolate Cake with Cinnamon

Cuts into 10 slices

50 g/2 oz cocoa powder
1 tsp ground cinnamon
225 g/8 oz self-raising flour
225 g/8 oz unsalted butter or margarine
225 g/8 oz caster sugar
4 large eggs

For the filling and topping:
125 g/4 oz white chocolate
50 ml/2 fl oz double cream
25 g/1 oz dark chocolate

1. Preheat the oven to 190°C/375°F/Gas Mark 5, 10 minutes before baking. Lightly oil and line the base of two 20.5 cm/ 8 inch sandwich tins with greaseproof paper or baking parchment. Sift the cocoa powder, cinnamon and flour together and reserve.

2. In a large bowl cream the butter or margarine and sugar, until light and fluffy. Beat in the eggs a little at a time until they are all incorporated and the mixture is smooth. (If it looks curdled at any point beat in 1 tablespoon of the sifted flour.)

3. Using a rubber spatula or metal spoon, fold the sifted flour and cocoa powder into the egg mixture until mixed well.

4. Divide between the two prepared cake tins, and level the surface. Bake in the preheated oven for 25–30 minutes, until springy to the touch and a skewer inserted into the centre of the cake comes out clean. Turn out on to a wire rack to cool.

5. To make the filling, coarsely break the white chocolate and heat the cream very gently in a small saucepan. Add the broken chocolate, stirring until melted. Leave to cool, then using half of the cooled white chocolate sandwich the cakes together.

6. Top the cake with the remaining cooled white chocolate. Coarsely grate the dark chocolate over the top and serve.

Dark Chocolate Layered Torte

Cuts into 10–12 slices

175 g/6 oz butter
1 tbsp instant coffee granules
150 g/ 5 oz dark chocolate
350 g/12 oz caster sugar
150 g/5 oz self-raising flour
125 g/4 oz plain flour
2 tbsp cocoa powder
2 medium eggs
1 tsp vanilla extract

For the filling and covering:
215 g/7½ oz dark chocolate, melted
125 g/4 oz butter, melted
40 g/1½ oz icing sugar, sifted
2 tsp raspberry jam
2½ tbsp chocolate liqueur
100 g/3½ oz toasted flaked almonds

1. Preheat the oven to 150°C/300°F/Gas Mark 2, 10 minutes before baking. Lightly oil and line a 23 cm/9 inch square cake tin.

2. Melt the butter in a saucepan, remove from the heat and stir in the coffee granules and 225 ml/8 fl oz hot water. Add the dark chocolate and sugar and stir until smooth, then pour into a bowl.

3. In another bowl, sift together the flours and cocoa powder. Using an electric mixer, whisk the sifted mixture into the chocolate mixture until smooth.

4. Beat in the eggs and vanilla extract. Pour into the tin and bake in the oven for 1¼ hours or until firm. Leave for at least 5 minutes before turning out onto a wire rack to cool.

5. For the filling, mix together 200 g/7 oz of the melted chocolate with the butter and icing sugar and beat until smooth. Leave to cool, then beat again. Reserve 4–5 tablespoons of the mixture.

6. Cut the cooled cake in half to make two rectangles, then split each rectangle in three horizontally. Place one cake layer on a plate and spread thinly with the jam, then a thin layer of dark chocolate filling. Top with a second cake layer and sprinkle with a little liqueur, then spread with filling. Repeat with the remaining cake layers, liqueur and filling.

7. Chill in the refrigerator for 2–3 hours or until firm. Cover the cake with the reserved chocolate filling and press the flaked almonds into the sides of the cake.

8. Place the remaining melted chocolate in a nonstick baking parchment piping bag. Snip a small hole in the tip and pipe thin lines 2 cm/¾ inch apart crossways over the cake. Drag a cocktail stick lengthways through the icing in alternating directions to create a feathered effect. Serve.

Chocolate Orange Fudge Cake

Cuts into 8–10 slices

60 g/2½ oz cocoa powder
grated zest of 1 orange
350 g/12 oz self-raising flour
2 tsp baking powder
1 tsp bicarbonate of soda
½ tsp salt
225 g/8 oz light soft brown sugar
175 g/6 oz butter, softened
3 medium eggs
1 tsp vanilla extract
250 ml/8 fl oz sour cream
6 tbsp butter
6 tbsp milk
thinly pared zest of 1 orange
6 tbsp cocoa powder
250 g/9 oz icing sugar, sifted

1. Preheat the oven to 180°C/350°F/Gas Mark 4, 10 minutes before baking. Lightly oil and line two 23 cm/9 inch round cake tins. Blend the cocoa powder and 50 ml/2 fl oz of boiling water until smooth. Stir in the orange zest and reserve. Sift together the flour, baking powder, bicarbonate of soda and salt, then reserve. Cream together the sugar and softened butter and beat in the eggs, 1 at a time, then the cocoa mixture and vanilla extract. Stir in the flour mixture and the cream in alternate spoonfuls.

2. Divide the mixture between the prepared tins and bake in the preheated oven for 35 minutes, or until the edges of the cake pull away from the tin and the tops spring back when lightly pressed. Cool in the tins for 10 minutes, then turn out onto wire racks until cold.

3. Gently heat together the butter and milk with the pared orange zest. Simmer for 10 minutes, stirring occasionally. Remove from the heat and discard the orange zest. Pour the warm orange and milk mixture into a large bowl and stir in the cocoa powder. Gradually beat in the sifted icing sugar and beat until the icing is smooth and spreadable. Place one cake onto a large serving plate. Top with about one-quarter of the icing, place the second cake on top, then cover the cake completely with the remaining icing. Serve.

Easy Chocolate Cake

Cuts into 8–10

75 g/3 oz dark chocolate, broken into squares
200 ml/7 fl oz milk
250 g/9 oz dark muscovado sugar
75 g/3 oz butter, softened
2 medium eggs, beaten
150 g/5 oz plain flour
½ tsp vanilla extract
1 tsp bicarbonate of soda
25 g/1 oz cocoa powder

For the topping and filling:
125 g/4 oz unsalted butter
225 g/8 oz icing sugar, sifted
175 g/6 oz fresh strawberries, halved
tiny mint sprigs, to decorate

1. Preheat the oven to 180°C/350°F/Gas Mark 4. Grease two 20.5 cm/8 inch round sandwich tins and line the bases with nonstick baking parchment. Place the chocolate, milk and 75 g/3 oz of the sugar in a heavy-based saucepan. Heat gently until the mixture has melted, then set aside to cool.

2. Place the butter and remaining sugar in a large bowl and whisk with an electric mixer until light and fluffy. Gradually whisk in the eggs, adding 1 teaspoon flour with each addition. Stir in the cooled melted chocolate mixture along with the vanilla extract. Sift in the flour, bicarbonate of soda and cocoa powder, then fold into the mixture until smooth.

3. Spoon the mixture into the tins and smooth level. Bake for about 30 minutes until a skewer inserted in the centre comes out clean. Turn out to cool on a wire rack.

4. To decorate, beat the butter with the icing sugar and 1 tablespoon warm water until light and fluffy, then place half in a piping bag fitted with a star nozzle. Spread half the buttercream over one sponge layer and scatter half the strawberries over it. Top with the other cake and spread the remaining buttercream over the top. Pipe a border of stars around the edge. Decorate with the remaining strawberries and mint sprigs.

Whole Orange & Chocolate Cake With Marmalade Cream

Cuts into 6–8 slices

1 small orange, scrubbed
2 medium eggs, separated, plus 1 whole egg
150 g/5 oz caster sugar
125 g/4 oz ground almonds
75 g/3 oz dark chocolate, melted

To decorate:
100 ml/3½ fl oz double cream
200 g/7 oz full fat soft cheese
25 g/1 oz icing sugar
2 tbsp orange marmalade
orange zest, to decorate

1. Preheat the oven to 180°C/350°F/Gas Mark 4, 10 minutes before baking. Lightly oil and line the base of a 900 g/2 lb loaf tin. Place the orange in a saucepan, cover with cold water and bring to the boil. Simmer for 1 hour until soft. Drain and leave to cool.

2. Place 2 egg yolks, 1 whole egg and the sugar in a heatproof bowl set over a saucepan of simmering water and whisk until doubled in bulk. Remove from the heat and whisk for 5 minutes until cooled. Cut the whole orange in half and discard the seeds, then place into a food processor or blender and blend to a purée. Carefully fold the purée into the egg yolk mixture with the ground almonds and melted chocolate.

3. Whisk the egg whites until stiff peaks form. Fold a large spoonful of the egg whites into the chocolate mixture, then fold the remaining egg whites into the mixture. Pour into the tin and bake in the oven for 50 minutes, or until firm and a skewer inserted into the centre comes out clean. Cool in the tin before turning out and discarding the lining paper.

4. Whip the double cream until just thickened. In another bowl, blend the soft cheese with the icing sugar and marmalade until smooth, then fold in the cream. Chill the marmalade cream in the refrigerator until required. Decorate with orange zest and serve cut in slices with the marmalade cream.

Apricot & Almond Layer Cake

Cuts into 8–10 slices

150 g/5 oz unsalted butter, softened
125 g/4 oz caster sugar
5 medium eggs, separated
150 g/5 oz dark chocolate, melted and cooled
150 g/5 oz self-raising flour, sifted
50 g/2 oz ground almonds
75 g/3 oz icing sugar, sifted
300 g/11 oz apricot jam
1 tbsp amaretto liqueur

For the icing:
125 g/4 oz unsalted butter, melted
125 g/4 oz dark chocolate, melted

1. Preheat the oven to 180°C/350°F/Gas Mark 4, 10 minutes before baking. Lightly oil and line two 23 cm/9 inch round cake tins. Cream the butter and sugar together until light and fluffy, then beat in the egg yolks, one at a time, beating well. Stir in the cooled chocolate with 1 tablespoon of cooled boiled water. Fold in the flour and ground almonds.

2. Whisk the egg whites until stiff, then gradually whisk in the icing sugar, beating well. Whisk until the egg whites are stiff and glossy, then fold the egg whites into the chocolate mixture in two batches. Divide the mixture between the tins and bake in the oven for 30–40 minutes or until firm. Leave for 5 minutes. Turn out onto wire racks to cool completely.

3. Split the cakes in half. Gently heat the jam, pass through a sieve and stir in the amaretto liqueur. Place one cake layer onto a plate. Spread with a little jam, then sandwich with the next layer. Repeat with all the layers and use any remaining jam to brush over the entire cake. Leave until the jam sets. Beat the butter and chocolate together until smooth, then cool at room temperature until thick. Cover the top and sides of the cake with the chocolate icing and leave to set before slicing and serving.

Fruit & Spice Chocolate Slice

Cuts into 10 slices

350 g/12 oz self-raising flour
1 tsp ground mixed spice
175 g/6 oz butter, chilled
125 g/4 oz dark chocolate, roughly chopped
125 g/4 oz dried mixed fruit
75 g/3 oz dried apricots, chopped
75 g/3 oz chopped mixed nuts
175 g/6 oz demerara sugar
2 medium eggs, lightly beaten
150 ml/¼ pint milk

1. Preheat the oven to 180°C/350°F/Gas Mark 4, 10 minutes before baking. Oil and line a deep 18 cm/7 inch square tin with nonstick baking parchment. Sift the flour and mixed spice into a bowl. Cut the butter into small squares and rub in until the mixture resembles fine breadcrumbs.

2. Add the chocolate, dried mixed fruit, apricots and nuts to the dry ingredients. Reserve 1 tablespoon of the sugar, then add the rest to the bowl and stir together. Add the eggs and half of the milk and mix together, then add enough of the remaining milk to give a soft dropping consistency.

3. Spoon the mixture into the prepared tin, level the surface with the back of a spoon and sprinkle with the reserved demerara sugar. Bake on the centre shelf of the preheated oven for 50 minutes. Cover the top with foil to prevent the cake from browning too much and bake for a further 30–40 minutes, or until it is firm to the touch and a skewer inserted into the centre of the cake comes out clean.

4. Leave the cake in the tin for 10 minutes to cool slightly, then turn out onto a wire rack and leave to cool completely. Cut into 10 slices and serve. Store in an airtight container.

Chocolate Mousse Cake

Cuts into 8–10 slices

450 g/1 lb dark chocolate, chopped
125 g/4 oz butter, softened
3 tbsp brandy
9 large eggs, separated
150 g/5 oz caster sugar
1 tbsp single cream and white chocolate curls, to decorate

For the chocolate glaze:
225 ml/8 fl oz double cream
225 g/8 oz dark chocolate, chopped
2 tbsp brandy

1. Preheat the oven to 180°C/350°F/Gas Mark 4, 10 minutes before baking. Lightly oil and line the bases of two 20.5 cm/8 inch springform tins with baking parchment.

2. Melt the chocolate and butter in a bowl over a saucepan of simmering water. Stir until smooth. Remove from the heat and stir in the brandy.

3. Whisk the egg yolks and the sugar, reserving 2 tablespoons of the sugar, until thick and creamy. Slowly beat in the chocolate mixture until smooth and well blended.

4. Whisk the egg whites until soft peaks form, then sprinkle over the remaining sugar and continue whisking until stiff but not dry. Fold a large spoonful of the egg whites into the chocolate mixture. Fold in the remaining egg whites.

5. Divide two thirds of the mixture between the tins, tapping to distribute the mixture evenly. Reserve the last third of the chocolate mousse mixture for the filling. Bake in the oven for about 20 minutes, or until the cakes are risen and set. Remove and cool for at least 1 hour.

6. Loosen the edges of the cake layers with a knife. Using the fingertips, lightly press the crusty edges down. Pour the rest of the mousse over one layer, spreading until even. Carefully unclip the side, remove the other cake from the tin and gently invert on to the mousse, bottom side up to make a flat top layer. Discard the paper and chill for 4–6 hours, or until set.

7. For the glaze, melt the cream and chocolate with the brandy in a heavy-based saucepan and stir until smooth. Cool until thickened.

8. Unclip the side of the mousse cake and place on a wire rack. Pour over half the glaze and spread to cover. Allow to set, then decorate with chocolate curls. To serve, heat the remaining glaze and pour round each slice, and dot with cream.

Mocha Truffle Cake

Cuts into 8–10 slices

3 medium eggs
125 g/4 oz caster sugar
40 g/1½ oz cornflour
40 g/1½ oz self-raising flour
2 tbsp cocoa powder
2 tbsp milk
2 tbsp coffee liqueur
100 g/3½ oz white chocolate, melted and cooled
200 g/7 oz dark chocolate, melted and cooled
600 ml/1 pint double cream
200 g/7 oz milk chocolate
100 g/3½ oz unsalted butter

1. Preheat the oven to 180°C/350°F/Gas Mark 4, 10 minutes before cooking. Lightly oil and line a deep 23 cm/9 inch round cake tin. Beat the eggs and sugar in a bowl until thick and creamy. Sift together the cornflour, self-raising flour and cocoa powder and fold lightly into the egg mixture. Spoon into the tin and bake in the preheated oven for 30 minutes or until firm. Turn out onto a wire rack and leave until cold. Split the cold cake horizontally into two layers. Mix together the milk and coffee liqueur and brush onto the cake layers.

2. Stir the cooled white chocolate into one bowl and the cooled dark chocolate into another one. Whip the cream until soft peaks form, then divide between the two bowls and stir. Place layer of cake in a 23 cm/9 inch springform tin. Spread with half the white chocolate cream. Top with the dark chocolate cream, then the remaining white chocolate cream, finally place the remaining cake layer on top. Chill in the refrigerator for 4 hours or overnight until set.

3. Before serving, melt the milk chocolate and butter in a heatproof bowl over a saucepan of simmering water. Stir until smooth. Remove from the heat and leave until thick enough to spread. Cover the top and sides of the cake. Leave to set, then chill in the refrigerator. Cut into slices and serve.

Rich Devil's Food Cake

Cuts into 12–16 slices

450 g/1 lb plain flour
1 tbsp bicarbonate of soda
½ tsp salt
75 g/3 oz cocoa powder
300 ml/½ pint milk
150 g/5 oz butter, softened
400 g/14 oz soft dark brown sugar
2 tsp vanilla extract
4 large eggs

For the chocolate fudge frosting:
275 g/10 oz caster sugar
½ tsp salt
125 g/4 oz dark chocolate, chopped
225 ml/8 fl oz milk
2 tbsp golden syrup
125 g/4 oz butter, diced
2 tsp vanilla extract

1. Preheat the oven to 180°C/350°F/Gas Mark 4, 10 minutes before baking. Lightly oil and line the bases of three 23 cm/9 inch cake tins with greaseproof paper or baking parchment. Sift the flour, bicarbonate of soda and salt into a bowl. Sift the cocoa powder into another bowl, gradually whisking in a little milk to form a paste. Continue whisking in the milk until a smooth mixture is formed.

2. Beat the butter, sugar and vanilla extract until light and fluffy then gradually beat in the eggs, beating well after each addition. Stir in the flour and cocoa mixtures alternately in three or four batches. Divide the mixture evenly among the three tins, smoothing the surfaces evenly. Bake in the preheated oven for 25-35 minutes, until cooked and firm to the touch. Remove, cool and turn out onto a wire rack. Discard the lining paper.

3. To make the frosting, put the sugar, salt and chocolate into a heavy-based saucepan and stir in the milk until blended. Add the golden syrup and butter. Bring the mixture to the boil over a medium-high heat, stirring to help dissolve the sugar. Boil for 1 minute, stirring constantly. Remove from the heat, stir in the vanilla extract and cool. When cool, whisk until thickened and slightly lightened in colour. Sandwich the three cake layers together with about a third of the frosting, placing the third cake layer with the flat side up.

4. Transfer to a serving plate and spread the remaining frosting over the top and sides. Swirl the top to create a decorative effect and serve.

Chocolate & Coconut Cake

Cuts into 8 slices

125 g/4 oz dark chocolate, roughly chopped
175 g/6 oz butter or margarine
175 g/6 oz caster sugar
3 medium eggs, beaten
175 g/6 oz self-raising flour
1 tbsp cocoa powder
50 g/2 oz desiccated coconut

For the frosting:
125 g/4 oz butter or margarine
2 tbsp creamed coconut
225 g/8 oz icing sugar
25 g/1 oz desiccated coconut, lightly toasted

1. Preheat the oven to 180°C/350°F/Gas Mark 4, 10 minutes before baking. Melt the chocolate in a small bowl placed over a saucepan of gently simmering water, ensuring that the base of the bowl does not touch the water. When the chocolate has melted, stir until smooth and allow to cool.

2. Lightly oil and line the bases of two 18 cm/7 inch sandwich tins with greaseproof paper or baking parchment. In a large bowl beat the butter or margarine and sugar together with a wooden spoon until light and creamy. Beat in the eggs a little at a time, then stir in the melted chocolate.

3. Sift the flour and cocoa powder together and gently fold into the chocolate mixture with a metal spoon or rubber spatula. Add the desiccated coconut and mix lightly. Divide between the two prepared tins and smooth the tops.

4. Bake in the preheated oven for 25–30 minutes, or until a skewer comes out clean when inserted into the centre of the cake. Allow to cool in the tin for 5 minutes, then turn out, discard the lining paper and leave on a wire rack until cold.

5. Beat together the butter or margarine and creamed coconut until light. Add the icing sugar and mix well. Spread half of the icing on one cake and press the cakes together. Spread the remaining icing over the top, sprinkle with the coconut and serve.

Chocolate Buttermilk Cake

Cuts into 8–10 slices

175 g/6 oz butter
1 tsp vanilla extract
350 g/12 oz caster sugar
4 medium eggs, separated
100 g/3½ oz self-raising flour
40 g/1½ oz cocoa powder
175 ml/6 fl oz buttermilk
200 g/7 oz dark chocolate
100 g/3½ oz butter
300 ml/½ pint double cream

1. Preheat the oven to 180°C/350°F/Gas Mark 4, 10 minutes before baking. Lightly oil and line a deep 23 cm/9 inch round cake tin. Cream together the butter, vanilla extract and sugar until light and fluffy, then beat in the egg yolks, 1 at a time.

2. Sift together the flour and cocoa powder and fold into the egg mixture together with the buttermilk. Whisk the egg whites until soft peaks form and fold carefully into the chocolate mixture in two batches. Spoon the mixture into the prepared tin and bake in the preheated oven for 1 hour or until firm. Cool slightly, then turn out onto a wire rack and leave until completely cold.

3. Place the chocolate and butter together in a heatproof bowl set over a saucepan of simmering water and heat until melted. Stir until smooth, then leave at room temperature until the chocolate is thick enough to spread.

4. Split the cake horizontally in half. Use some of the chocolate mixture to sandwich the two halves together. Spread and decorate the top of the cake with the remaining chocolate mixture. Finally, whip the cream until soft peaks form and use to spread around the sides of the cake. Chill in the refrigerator until required. Serve cut into slices. Store in the refrigerator.

Chocolate Brazil Nut & Polenta Squares

Cuts into 9 squares

150 g/5 oz shelled Brazil nuts
150 g/5 oz butter, softened
150 g/5 oz soft light brown sugar
2 medium eggs, lightly beaten
75 g/3 oz plain flour
25 g/1 oz cocoa powder
¼ tsp ground cinnamon
1 tsp baking powder
pinch salt
5 tbsp milk
65 g/2½ oz instant polenta

1. Preheat the oven to 180°C/350°F/Gas Mark 4, 10 minutes before baking. Oil and line a deep 18 cm/7 inch square tin with nonstick baking parchment. Finely chop 50 g/2 oz of the Brazil nuts and reserve. Roughly chop the remainder. Cream the butter and sugar together until light and fluffy. Gradually add the eggs, beating well between each addition.

2. Sift the flour, cocoa powder, cinnamon, baking powder and salt into the creamed mixture and gently fold in using a large metal spoon or spatula. Add the milk, polenta and the 75 g/3 oz of roughly chopped Brazil nuts. Fold into the mixture.

3. Turn the mixture into the tin, levelling the surface with the back of the spoon. Sprinkle the reserved Brazil nuts over the top. Bake the cake on the centre shelf of the oven for 45–50 minutes, or until well risen and lightly browned and when a skewer inserted into the centre of the cake comes out clean.

4. Leave the cake in the tin for 10 minutes to cool slightly, then turn out onto a wire rack and leave to cool completely. Cut the cake into nine equal squares and serve. Store in an airtight container.

Chocolate Walnut Squares

Cuts into 24 squares

125 g/4 oz butter
150 g/5 oz dark chocolate, broken into squares
450 g/1 lb caster sugar
1/2 tsp vanilla extract
200 g/7 oz plain flour
75 g/3 oz self-raising flour
50 g/2 oz cocoa powder
225 g/8 oz mayonnaise, at room temperature

For the chocolate glaze:
125 g/4 oz dark chocolate, broken into squares
40 g/1½ oz unsalted butter
24 walnut halves
1 tbsp icing sugar, for dusting

1. Preheat the oven to 170°C/325°F/Gas Mark 3, 10 minutes before baking. Oil and line a 28 x 18 x 5 cm/11 x 7 x 2 inch cake tin with nonstick baking parchment. Place the butter, chocolate, sugar, vanilla extract and 225 ml/8 fl oz cold water in a heavy-based saucepan. Heat gently, stirring occasionally, until the chocolate and butter have melted, but do not allow to boil.

2. Sift the flours and cocoa powder into a large bowl and make a well in the centre. Add the mayonnaise and about one third of the chocolate mixture and beat until smooth. Gradually beat in the remaining chocolate mixture. Pour into the prepared tin and bake on the centre shelf of the preheated oven for 1 hour, or until slightly risen and firm to the touch. Place the tin on a wire rack and leave to cool. Remove the cake from the tin and peel off the baking parchment.

3. For the chocolate glaze, place the chocolate and butter in a small saucepan with 1 tablespoon water and heat gently, stirring occasionally until melted and smooth. Leave to cool until thickened, then spread evenly over the cake. Chill in the refrigerator for about 5 minutes, then mark into 24 squares. Lightly dust the walnuts with a little icing sugar and place one on the top of each square. Cut the cake into pieces and store in an airtight container until ready to serve.

Cranberry & White Chocolate Cake

Cuts into 4 slices

225 g/8 oz butter, softened
250 g/9 oz full fat soft cheese
150 g/5 oz light soft brown sugar
200 g/7 oz caster sugar
grated zest of ½ orange
1 tsp vanilla extract
4 medium eggs
375 g/13 oz plain flour
2 tsp baking powder
200 g/7 oz cranberries, thawed if frozen
225 g/8 oz white chocolate, coarsely chopped
2 tbsp orange juice

1. Preheat the oven to 180°C/350°F/Gas Mark 4, 10 minutes before baking. Lightly oil and flour a 23 cm/9 inch kugelhopf tin or ring tin. Using an electric mixer, cream the butter and cheese with the sugars until light and fluffy. Add the grated orange zest and vanilla extract and beat until smooth, then beat in the eggs, 1 at a time.

2. Sift the flour and baking powder together and stir into the creamed mixture, beating well after each addition. Fold in the cranberries and 175 g/6 oz of the white chocolate. Spoon into the prepared tin and bake in the preheated oven for 1 hour, or until firm and a skewer inserted into the centre comes out clean. Cool in the tin before turning out onto on a wire rack.

3. Melt the remaining white chocolate, stir until smooth, then stir in the orange juice and leave to cool until thickened. Transfer the cake to a serving plate and spoon over the white chocolate and orange glaze. Leave to set.

Chocolate Box Cake

Cuts into 16 slices

175 g/6 oz self-raising flour
1 tsp baking powder
175 g/6 oz caster sugar
175 g/6 oz butter, softened
3 large eggs
25 g/1 oz cocoa powder

For the chocolate box:
275 g/10 oz dark chocolate
150 g/5 oz apricot preserve

For the topping:
450 ml/¾ pint double cream
275 g/10 oz dark chocolate, melted
2 tbsp brandy
1 tsp cocoa powder to decorate

1. Preheat the oven to 180°C/350°F/Gas Mark 4, 10 minutes before baking. Lightly oil and flour a 20.5 cm/8 inch square cake tin. Sift the flour and baking powder into a large bowl and stir in the sugar. Using an electric mixer, beat in the butter and eggs. Blend the cocoa powder with 1 tablespoon water, then beat into the creamed mixture. Turn into the tin and bake for about 25 minutes, or until well risen and cooked. Remove and cool before removing the cake from the tin.

2. For the chocolate box, break the chocolate into small pieces, place in a heatproof bowl over a saucepan of gently simmering water and leave until soft. Stir occasionally until melted and smooth. Line a Swiss roll tin with nonstick baking parchment then pour in the melted chocolate, tilting the tin to level. Leave until set, then turn out onto a chopping board and strip off the paper. Cut into four strips, the same length as the cooked sponge, using a large sharp knife that has been dipped into hot water. Gently heat the apricot preserve and sieve to remove lumps. Brush over the top and sides of the cake. Carefully place the chocolate strips around the cake sides and press lightly. Leave to set for at least 10 minutes.

3. For the topping, whisk the cream to soft peaks and quickly fold into the melted chocolate with the brandy. Spoon the mixture into a pastry bag with a star nozzle and pipe rosettes or shells over the surface. Dust with cocoa power and serve.

Chocolate Chiffon Cake

Cuts into 10–12 slices

50 g/2 oz cocoa powder
300 g/11 oz self-raising flour
550 g/1 lb 3 oz caster sugar
7 medium eggs, separated
125 ml/4 fl oz vegetable oil
1 tsp vanilla extract

For the filling and glaze:
175 g/6 oz butter
275 g/10 oz icing sugar, sifted
2 tbsp cocoa powder, sifted
2 tbsp brandy
75 g/3 oz walnuts
200 g/7 oz dark chocolate, melted

1. Preheat the oven to 170°C/325°F/Gas Mark 3, 10 minutes before serving. Lightly oil and line a 23 cm/9 inch round cake tin. Lightly oil a baking sheet. Blend the cocoa powder with 175 ml/6 fl oz boiling water and leave to cool. Place the flour and 350 g/12 oz of the caster sugar in a large bowl, and add the cocoa mixture, egg yolks, oil and vanilla extract. Whisk until smooth and lighter in colour. Whisk the egg whites in a clean, grease-free bowl until soft peaks form, then fold into the cocoa mixture. Pour into the tin and bake in the preheated oven for 1 hour or until firm. Leave for 5 minutes, then turn out onto a wire rack to cool.

2. For the icing, cream 125 g/4 oz of the butter with the icing sugar, cocoa powder and brandy until smooth, then reserve. Melt the remaining butter and blend with 150 g/5 oz of the melted chocolate. Stir until smooth, leave until thickened.

3. Place the remaining caster sugar into a heavy-based saucepan over a low heat. Heat until the sugar has melted and is a deep golden brown. Add the walnuts and the remaining melted chocolate to the melted sugar. Pour onto the baking sheet. Leave until cold and brittle, then chop finely. Reserve. Split the cake into three layers, place one layer onto a plate and spread with half of the icing. Top with a second cake layer and spread with the remaining icing. Arrange the last cake layer on top. Cover the cake with the thickened chocolate glaze. Sprinkle with the walnut praline and serve.

Everyday Cakes

Maple, Pecan & Lemon Loaf

Cuts into 12 slices

350 g/12 oz plain flour
1 tsp baking powder
175 g/6 oz butter, cubed
75 g/3 oz caster sugar
125 g/4 oz pecan nuts, roughly chopped
3 medium eggs
1 tbsp milk
finely grated zest of 1 lemon
5 tbsp maple syrup

For the icing:
75 g/3 oz icing sugar
1 tbsp lemon juice
25 g/1 oz pecans, roughly chopped

1. Preheat the oven to 170°C/325°F/Gas Mark 3, 10 minutes before baking. Lightly oil and line the base of a 900 g/ 2 lb loaf tin with non-stick baking parchment.

2. Sift the flour and baking powder into a large bowl. Rub in the butter until the mixture resembles fine breadcrumbs. Stir in the caster sugar and pecan nuts. In a separate bowl, beat the eggs together with the milk and lemon zest. Stir in the maple syrup. Add to the dry ingredients and gently stir in until mixed thoroughly to make a soft dropping consistency.

3. Spoon the mixture into the prepared tin and level the top with the back of a spoon. Bake on the middle shelf of the preheated oven for 50–60 minutes, or until the cake is well risen and lightly browned. If a skewer inserted into the centre comes out clean, then the cake is ready.

4. Leave the cake in the tin for about 10 minutes, then turn out and leave to cool on a wire rack. Carefully remove the lining paper.

5. Sift the icing sugar into a small bowl and stir in the lemon juice to make a smooth icing. Drizzle the icing over the top of the loaf, then scatter with the chopped pecans. Leave to set, slice thickly and serve.

Fat-Free Sponge

Cuts into 8 slices

3 medium eggs
175 g/6 oz caster sugar, plus extra for dusting
125 g/4 oz self-raising flour, plus extra for dusting

To decorate:
150 ml/¼ pint low-fat whipping cream, or low-fat crème fraîche or yogurt
2 tbsp lemon curd
125 g/4 oz blueberries
zest of 1 lemon, cut into long thin strips

1. Preheat the oven to 190°C/375°F/Gas Mark 5. Grease two nonstick 18 cm/7 inch sandwich tins, line with nonstick baking parchment, dust with a mixture of sugar and flour.

2. Put the eggs and sugar in a large bowl and stand this over a pan of hot water. Whisk the eggs and sugar until doubled in volume and the mixture is thick enough to leave a trail on the surface of the batter when the whisk is lifted away.

3. Remove the bowl from the heat and continue whisking for a further 5 minutes until the mixture is cool. Sift half the flour over the mixture and fold in very lightly, using a large metal spoon. Sift in the remaining flour and fold in the same way.

4. Pour the mixture into the prepared tins and tilt them to spread the mixture evenly. Bake for 15–20 minutes until well risen and firm and the cakes are beginning to shrink away from the sides of the tins. Leave to stand for 2 minutes, then turn out to cool on a wire rack.

5. To decorate, whip the cream, if using, and spread half the cream (or crème fraîche or yogurt) over one cake. Swirl 1 tablespoon of lemon curd into the cream, crème fraîche or yogurt and scatter over half the blueberries. Place the other cake on top and swirl over the remaining cream/yogurt. Swirl over 1 tablespoon of lemon curd and sprinkle with the remaining berries. Scatter the strips of lemon zest over the top.

Lemony Coconut Cake

Cuts into 10–12 slices

75 g/10 oz plain flour
2 tbsp cornflour
1 tbsp baking powder
1 tsp salt
150 g/5 oz white vegetable fat or soft margarine
275 g/10 oz caster sugar
grated zest of 2 lemons
1 tsp vanilla extract
3 large eggs
150 ml/¼ pint milk
4 tbsp Malibu or rum
450 g/1 lb jar lemon curd
lime zest, to decorate

For the frosting:
275 g/10 oz caster sugar
125 ml/4 fl oz water
1 tbsp glucose
¼ tsp salt
1 tsp vanilla extract
3 large egg whites
75 g/3 oz shredded coconut

1. Preheat the oven to 180°C/350°F/Gas Mark 4, 10 minutes before baking. Lightly oil and flour two 20.5 cm/8 inch nonstick cake tins.

2. Sift the flour, cornflour, baking powder and salt into a bowl and add the fat or margarine, sugar, lemon zest, vanilla extract, eggs and milk. With an electric mixer on a low speed, beat until blended, adding a little extra milk if the mixture is very stiff. Increase the speed to medium and beat for about 2 minutes.

3. Divide the mixture between the tins and smooth the tops. Bake in the oven for 20–25 minutes, or until the cakes feel firm. Remove and cool before removing from the tins.

4. Put all the frosting ingredients, except the coconut, into a heatproof bowl placed over a saucepan of simmering water.

5. Using an electric mixer, blend the ingredients on a low speed. Increase the speed to high and beat for 7 minutes, until the whites are stiff and glossy. Remove the bowl from the heat and continue beating until cool. Cover with clingfilm.

6. Split the cake layers horizontally in half and sprinkle each cut surface with the rum. Sandwich the cakes together with the lemon curd and press lightly.

7. Spread the top and sides with the frosting, swirling and peaking the top. Sprinkle the coconut over the top and gently press on to the sides to cover. Decorate with the lime zest and serve.

Lemon Drizzle Cake

Cuts into 16 squares

125 g/4 oz butter or margarine
175 g/6 oz caster sugar
2 large eggs
175 g/6 oz self-raising flour
2 lemons, preferably unwaxed
50 g/2 oz granulated sugar

1. Preheat the oven to 180°C/350°F/Gas Mark 4, 10 minutes before baking. Lightly oil and line the base of an 18 cm/ 7 inch square cake tin with baking parchment.

2. In a large bowl, cream the butter or margarine and sugar together until soft and fluffy. Beat the eggs, then gradually add a little of the egg to the creamed mixture, adding 1 tablespoon of flour after each addition.

3. Finely grate the zest from 1 of the lemons and stir into the creamed mixture, beating well until smooth. Squeeze the juice from the lemon, strain, then stir into the mixture.

4. Spoon into the prepared tin, level the surface and bake in the preheated oven for 25–30 minutes. Using a zester remove the peel from the last lemon and mix with 25 g/ 1 oz of the granulated sugar and reserve.

5. Squeeze the juice into a small saucepan. Add the rest of the granulated sugar to the lemon juice in the saucepan and heat gently, stirring occasionally. When the sugar has dissolved simmer gently for 3–4 minutes until syrupy.

6. With a cocktail stick or fine skewer prick the cake all over.

7. Sprinkle the lemon zest and sugar over the top of the cake, drizzle over the syrup and leave to cool in the tin. Cut the cake into squares and serve.

Lemon-Iced Ginger Squares

Cuts into 12 slices

225 g/8 oz caster sugar
50 g/2 oz butter, melted
2 tbsp black treacle
2 medium egg whites, lightly whisked
225 g/8 oz plain flour
1 tsp bicarbonate of soda
¼ tsp ground ginger
½ tsp ground cloves
1 tsp ground cinnamon
pinch salt
225 ml/8 fl oz buttermilk
175 g/6 oz icing sugar
lemon juice

1. Preheat the oven to 200°C/400°F/Gas Mark 6, 15 minutes before baking. Lightly oil a 20.5 cm/8 inch square cake tin and sprinkle with a little flour.

2. Mix together the caster sugar, butter and treacle. Stir in the egg whites.

3. Mix together the flour, bicarbonate of soda, ginger, cloves, cinnamon, and salt. Stir the flour mixture and buttermilk alternately into the butter mixture until blended well. Spoon into the prepared tin and bake in the oven for 35 minutes, or until a skewer inserted into the centre of the cake comes out clean.

4. Remove from the oven and allow to cool for 5 minutes in the tin before turning out on to a wire rack over a large plate. Using a cocktail stick make holes on the top of the cake.

5. Meanwhile, mix together the icing sugar with enough lemon juice to make a smooth pourable icing. Carefully pour the icing over the hot cake, then leave until cold. Cut the ginger cake into squares and serve.

Easy Sponge Cake

Cuts into 8 slices

225 g/8 oz soft margarine
225 g/8 oz caster sugar
4 medium eggs
1 tsp vanilla extract
225 g/8 oz self-raising flour
1 tsp baking powder
icing sugar, to dust

For the filling:
4 tbsp seedless raspberry jam
100 ml/3½ fl oz double cream

1. Preheat the oven to 180°C/350°F/Gas Mark 4. Grease two 20.5 cm/8 inch sandwich tins and line the bases with nonstick baking parchment.

2. Place the margarine, sugar, eggs and vanilla extract in a large bowl and sift in the flour and baking powder. Beat for about 2 minutes until smooth and blended, then divide between the tins and smooth level.

3. Bake for about 25 minutes until golden, well risen and the tops of the cakes spring back when lightly touched with a fingertip. Leave to cool in the tins for 2 minutes, then turn out onto a wire rack to cool. When cold, peel away the baking parchment.

4. When completely cold, spread one cake with jam and place on a serving plate. Whip the cream until it forms soft peaks, then spread on the underside of the other cake. Sandwich the two cakes together and sift a little icing sugar over the top.

Coffee & Pecan Cake

Cuts into 8 slices

175 g/6 oz self-raising flour
125 g/4 oz butter or margarine
175 g/6 oz golden caster sugar
1 tbsp instant coffee powder or granules
2 large eggs
50 g/2 oz pecans, roughly chopped

For the frosting:
1 tsp instant coffee powder or granules
1 tsp cocoa powder
75 g/3 oz unsalted butter, softened
175 g/6 oz icing sugar, sifted
whole pecans, to decorate

1. Preheat the oven to 190°C/375°F/Gas Mark 5, 10 minutes before baking. Lightly oil and line the bases of two 18 cm/ 7 inch sandwich tins with greaseproof paper or baking parchment. Sift the flour and reserve.

2. Beat the butter or margarine and sugar together until light and creamy. Dissolve the coffee in 2 tablespoons of hot water and allow to cool.

3. Lightly mix the eggs with the coffee liquid. Gradually beat into the creamed butter and sugar, adding a little of the sifted flour with each addition.

4. Fold in the pecans, then divide the mixture between the prepared tins and bake in the preheated oven for 20–25 minutes, or until well risen and firm to the touch. Leave to cool in the tins for 5 minutes before turning out and cooling on a wire rack.

5. To make the icing, blend together the coffee and cocoa powder with enough boiling water to make a stiff paste. Beat into the butter and icing sugar.

6. Sandwich the 2 cakes together using half of the icing. Spread the remaining icing over the top of the cake and decorate with the whole pecans to serve. Store in an airtight tin.

Citrus Cake

Cuts into 6 slices

175 g/6 oz golden caster sugar
175 g/6 oz butter or margarine
3 medium eggs
2 tbsp orange juice
175 g/6 oz self-raising flour
finely grated zest of 2 oranges
5 tbsp lemon curd
125 g/4 oz icing sugar
finely grated zest of 1 lemon
1 tbsp freshly squeezed lemon juice

1. Preheat the oven to 190°C/375°F/Gas Mark 5, 10 minutes before baking. Lightly oil and line the base of a round 20.5 cm/8 inch deep cake tin with baking parchment.

2. In a large bowl, cream the sugar and butter or margarine together until light and fluffy. Whisk the eggs together and beat into the creamed mixture a little at a time.

3. Beat in the orange juice with 1 tablespoon of the flour. Sift the remaining flour on to a large plate several times, then with a metal spoon or rubber spatula, fold into the creamed mixture.

4. Spoon into the prepared cake tin. Stir the finely grated orange zest into the lemon curd and dot randomly across the top of the mixture.

5. Using a fine skewer swirl the lemon curd through the cake mixture. Bake in the preheated oven for 35 minutes, until risen and golden. Allow to cool for 5 minutes in the tin, then turn out carefully on to a wire rack.

6. Sift the icing sugar into a bowl, add the grated lemon zest and juice and stir well to mix. When the cake is cold cover the top with the icing and serve.

Toffee Apple Cake

Cuts into 8 slices

2 small eating apples, peeled
4 tbsp soft dark brown sugar
175 g/6 oz butter or margarine
175 g/6 oz caster sugar
3 medium eggs
175 g/6 oz self-raising flour
150 ml/¼ pint double cream
2 tbsp icing sugar
½ tsp vanilla extract
½ tsp ground cinnamon

1. Preheat the oven to 180°C/350°F/Gas Mark 4, 10 minutes before baking time. Lightly oil and line the bases of two 20.5 cm/8 inch sandwich tins with greaseproof paper or baking parchment.

2. Thinly slice the apples and toss in the brown sugar until well coated. Arrange them over the base of the prepared tins and reserve.

3. Cream together the butter or margarine and caster sugar until light and fluffy. Beat the eggs together in a small bowl and gradually beat them into the creamed mixture, beating well between each addition.

4. Sift the flour into the mixture and using a metal spoon or rubber spatula, fold in.

5. Divide the mixture between the two cake tins and level the surface. Bake in the preheated oven for 25–30 minutes, until golden and well risen. Leave in the tins to cool.

6. Lightly whip the cream with 1 tablespoon of the icing sugar and vanilla extract.

7. Sandwich the cakes together with the cream. Mix the remaining icing sugar and ground cinnamon together, sprinkle over the top of the cake and serve.

Honey Cake

Cuts into 6 slices

50 g/2 oz butter
25 g/1 oz caster sugar
125 g/4 oz clear honey
175 g/6 oz plain flour
½ tsp bicarbonate of soda
½ tsp mixed spice
1 medium egg
2 tbsp milk
25 g/1 oz flaked almonds
1 tbsp clear honey, to drizzle

1. Preheat the oven to 180°C/350°F/Gas Mark 4, 10 minutes before baking. Lightly oil and line the base of an 18 cm/7 inch deep round cake tin with lightly oiled greaseproof paper or baking parchment.

2. In a saucepan gently heat the butter, sugar and honey until the butter has just melted.

3. Sift the flour, bicarbonate of soda and mixed spice together into a bowl.

4. Beat the egg and the milk until mixed thoroughly.

5. Make a well in the centre of the sifted flour and pour in the melted butter and honey. Using a wooden spoon, beat well, gradually drawing in the flour from the sides of the bowl. When all the flour has been beaten in, add the egg mixture and mix thoroughly. Pour into the prepared tin and sprinkle with the flaked almonds.

6. Bake in the preheated oven for 30–35 minutes, or until well risen and golden brown and a skewer inserted into the centre of the cake comes out clean.

7. Remove from the oven, cool for a few minutes in the tin before turning out and leaving to cool on a wire rack. Drizzle with the remaining tablespoon of honey and serve.

Toffee Walnut Roll

Cuts into 10–12 slices

4 large eggs, separated
½ tsp cream of tartar
125 g/4 oz icing sugar,
  plus extra to dust
½ tsp vanilla extract
125 g/4 oz self-raising flour

For the toffee walnut filling:
2 tbsp plain flour
150 ml/¼ pint milk
5 tbsp golden or maple syrup
2 large egg yolks, beaten
100 g/3½ oz walnuts or
  pecans, toasted and chopped
300 ml/½ pint double cream, whipped

1. Preheat the oven to 190°C/375°F/Gas Mark 5, 10 minutes before baking. Lightly oil and line a Swiss roll tin. Beat the egg whites and cream of tartar until softly peaking. Gradually beat in 50 g/2 oz of the icing sugar until stiff peaks form.

2. In another bowl, beat the egg yolks with the remaining icing sugar until thick. Beat in the vanilla extract. Fold in the flour and egg whites alternately. Do not over mix. Spoon into the tin and spread evenly. Bake in the oven for 12 minutes, or until golden and the cake springs back when pressed with a finger.

3. Lay a tea towel on a work surface and lay a piece of baking parchment about 33 cm/13 inches long on the towel and dust with icing sugar. As soon as the cake is cooked turn out on to the paper. Peel off the lining paper and cut off the crisp edges of the cake. Starting at one narrow end, roll the cake with the paper and towel. Transfer to a wire rack and cool completely.

4. For the filling, put the flour, milk and syrup into a saucepan and place over a gentle heat. Bring to the boil, whisking until thick and smooth. Remove from the heat and slowly beat into the beaten egg yolks.

5. Pour the mixture back into the saucepan and cook over a low heat until it thickens. Strain the mixture into a bowl and stir in the nuts. Cool, stirring occasionally, then fold in about half of the whipped cream.

6. Unroll the cake and spread the filling over. Re-roll, decorate with the remaining cream. Sprinkle with the icing sugar. Serve.

Fruit Cake

Cuts into 10 slices

225 g/8 oz butter or margarine
200 g/7 oz soft brown sugar
finely grated zest of 1 orange
1 tbsp black treacle
3 large eggs, beaten
275 g/10 oz plain flour
¼ tsp ground cinnamon
½ tsp mixed spice
pinch freshly grated nutmeg
¼ tsp bicarbonate of soda
75 g/3 oz mixed peel
50 g/2 oz glacé cherries
125 g/4 oz raisins
125 g/4 oz sultanas
125 g/4 oz ready-to-eat dried apricots, chopped

1. Preheat the oven to 150°C/300°F/Gas Mark 2, 10 minutes before baking. Lightly oil and line a 23 cm/9 inch deep round cake tin with a double thickness of greaseproof paper.

2. In a large bowl cream together the butter or margarine, sugar and orange zest, until light and fluffy, then beat in the treacle. Beat in the eggs a little at a time, beating well between each addition. Reserve 1 tablespoon of the flour. Sift the remaining flour, the spices and bicarbonate of soda into the mixture.

3. Mix all the fruits and the reserved flour together, then stir into the cake mixture. Turn into the prepared tin and smooth the top, making a small hollow in the centre of the cake mixture. Bake in the preheated oven for 1 hour, then reduce the heat to 140°C/275°F/Gas Mark 1.

4. Bake for a further 1½ hours, or until cooked and a skewer inserted into the centre comes out clean. Leave to cool in the tin, then turn the cake out and serve. Otherwise, when cold store in an airtight tin.

Almond Cake

Cuts into 8 slices

225 g/8 oz butter or margarine
225 g/8 oz caster sugar
3 large eggs
1 tsp vanilla extract
1 tsp almond extract
125 g/4 oz self-raising flour
175 g/6 oz ground almonds
50 g/2 oz whole almonds, blanched
25 g/1 oz dark chocolate

1. Preheat the oven to 150°C/300°F/Gas Mark 2. Lightly oil and line the base of a 20.5 cm/8 inch deep round cake tin with greaseproof paper or baking parchment.

2. Cream together the butter or margarine and sugar with a wooden spoon until light and fluffy. Beat the eggs and extracts together. Gradually add to the sugar and butter mixture and mix well between each addition.

3. Sift the flour and mix with the ground almonds. Beat into the egg mixture until mixed well and smooth. Pour into the prepared cake tin.

4. Roughly chop the whole almonds and scatter over the cake before baking in the oven. Bake in the oven for 45 minutes, or until golden and risen and a skewer inserted into the centre of the cake comes out clean.

5. Remove from the tin and leave to cool on a wire rack. Melt the chocolate in a small bowl placed over a saucepan of gently simmering water, stirring until smooth and free of lumps.

6. Drizzle the melted chocolate over the cooled cake and serve once the chocolate has set.

Chestnut Cake

Cuts into 8–10 slices

175 g/6 oz butter, softened
175 g/6 oz caster sugar
250 g can sweetened chestnut purée
3 medium eggs, lightly beaten
175 g/6 oz plain flour
1 tsp baking powder
pinch ground cloves
1 tsp fennel seeds, crushed
75 g/3 oz raisins
50 g/2 oz pine nuts, toasted
125 g/4 oz icing sugar
5 tbsp lemon juice
pared strips of lemon zest, to decorate

1. Preheat oven to 150°C/300°F/Gas Mark 2. Oil and line a 23 cm/9 inch springform tin. Beat together the butter and sugar until light and fluffy. Add the chestnut purée and beat. Gradually add the eggs, beating after each addition. Sift in the flour with the baking powder and cloves. Add the fennel seeds and beat. The mixture should drop easily from a wooden spoon when tapped against the side of the bowl. If not, add a little milk.

2. Beat in the raisins and pine nuts. Spoon the mixture into the prepared tin and smooth the top. Transfer to the centre of the oven and bake in the preheated oven for 55–60 minutes, or until a skewer inserted in the centre of the cake comes out clean. Remove from the oven and leave in the tin.

3. Meanwhile, mix together the icing sugar and lemon juice in a small saucepan until smooth. Heat gently until hot, but not boiling. Using a cocktail stick or skewer, poke holes into the cake all over. Pour the hot syrup evenly over the cake and leave to soak into the cake. Decorate with pared strips of lemon and serve.

Double Marble Cake

Cuts into 8–10 slices

75 g/3 oz white chocolate
75 g/3 oz dark chocolate
175 g/6 oz caster sugar
175 g/6 oz butter
4 medium eggs, separated
125 g/4 oz plain flour, sifted
75 g/3 oz ground almonds

For the topping:
100 g/3½ oz white chocolate, chopped
100 g/3½ oz dark chocolate, chopped
100 ml/3½ fl oz double cream
200 g/7 oz unsalted butter

1. Preheat the oven to 180°C/350°F/Gas Mark 4, 10 minutes before baking. Lightly oil and line the base of a 20.5 cm/ 8 inch cake tin. Break both chocolates into small pieces, then place in two separate bowls placed over two pans of simmering water, ensuring that the bowls are not touching the water. Heat the chocolate until melted and smooth.

2. In a large bowl cream the sugar and butter together until light and fluffy. Beat in the egg yolks, 1 at a time and add a spoonful of flour after each addition. Stir in the ground almonds. In another bowl whisk the egg whites until stiff. Gently fold in the egg whites and the remaining sifted flour alternately into the almond mixture until all the flour and egg whites have been incorporated. Divide the mixture between two bowls. Gently stir the white chocolate into one bowl, then add the dark chocolate to the other bowl.

3. Place alternating spoonfuls of the chocolate mixtures in the prepared cake tin. Swirl the mixtures together to get a marbled effect, then tap the tin on the work surface to level the mixture. Bake in the oven for 40 minutes, or until cooked through, then leave to cool for 5 minutes in the tin, before turning out onto a wire rack to cool.

4. For the topping, melt half of the cream and butter with the dark chocolate and the other half with the white and stir both until smooth. Cool, whisk until thick and swirl both colours over the top of the cake to create a marbled effect.

Almond Fruit Cake

Cuts into 8–10 slices

400 g/14 oz mixed dried fruit
50 g/2 oz ground almonds
finely grated zest and juice of 1 lemon
150 g/5 oz butter, softened
150 g/5 oz natural golden caster sugar
3 medium eggs, beaten
125 g/4 oz plain flour
40 g/1½ oz whole blanched almonds

1. Preheat the oven to 180°C/350°F/Gas Mark 4. Grease and line the base of an 18 cm/7 inch deep round cake tin with nonstick baking parchment.

2. Place the dried fruits in a bowl and stir in the ground almonds to coat the dried fruit.

3. Grate the zest finely from the lemon into the bowl, then squeeze out 1 tablespoon of juice and add to the same bowl. In another bowl, beat the butter and sugar together until light and fluffy. Whisk in the eggs a little at a time, adding 1 teaspoon of flour with each addition.

4. Sift in the remaining flour, then add the fruit and almond mixture. Fold together with a large metal spoon until smooth. Spoon the mixture into the tin and make a dip in the centre with the back of a spoon. Arrange the almonds over the top in circles.

5. Bake for 1 hour, then reduce the heat to 150°C/300°F/Gas Mark 2 and bake for a further hour, or until a skewer inserted into the centre comes out clean. Cool in the tin for 5 minutes, then turn out to cool on a wire rack.

Buttery Passion Fruit Cake

Cuts into 8–10 slices

210 g/7½ oz plain flour
1 tsp baking powder
175 g/6 oz unsalted butter, softened
250 g/9 oz caster sugar, plus 1 tsp for sprinkling
grated zest of 1 orange
1 tsp vanilla extract
3 medium eggs, beaten
2 tbsp milk
6 ripe passion fruits
50 g/2 oz icing sugar, plus extra to dust

1. Preheat the oven to 180°C/350°F/Gas Mark 4, 10 minutes before baking. Lightly oil and line the base of a 23 x 12.5 cm/9 x 5 inch loaf tin with greaseproof paper. Sift the flour and baking powder into a bowl and reserve.

2. Beat the butter, sugar, orange zest and vanilla extract until light and fluffy, then gradually beat in the eggs, 1 tablespoon at a time, beating after each addition. If the mixture appears to curdle or separate, beat in a little of the flour mixture.

3. Fold in the flour mixture with the milk until just blended. Do not over mix. Spoon lightly into the prepared tin and smooth the top evenly. Sprinkle lightly with the teaspoon of caster sugar. Bake in the preheated oven for 55 minutes, or until well risen and golden brown. Remove from the oven and leave to cool for 15–20 minutes.

4. Cut the passion fruits in half. Scoop out the pulp into a sieve set over a bowl. Press the juice through. Stir in the icing sugar and stir to dissolve, adding a little extra sugar if needed.

5. Using a skewer, pierce holes all over the cake. Slowly spoon the fruit glaze over the cake and allow to seep in. Turn the cake out of the tin onto a wire rack and turn it back the right way up, discarding the lining paper. Dust with icing sugar and cool completely. Serve cold.

Luxury Carrot Cake

Cuts into 12 slices

275 g/10 oz plain flour
2 tsp baking powder
1 tsp bicarbonate of soda
1 tsp salt
2 tsp ground cinnamon
1 tsp ground ginger
200 g/7 oz dark soft brown sugar
100 g/3½ oz caster sugar
4 large eggs, beaten
250 ml/8 fl oz sunflower oil
1 tbsp vanilla extract
4 carrots, peeled and shredded (about 450 g/1 lb)
400-g can crushed pineapple, well drained
125 g/4 oz pecans or walnuts, toasted and chopped

For the frosting:
175 g/6 oz cream cheese, softened
50 g/2 oz butter, softened
1 tsp vanilla extract
225 g/8 oz icing sugar, sifted
1–2 tbsp milk

1. Preheat the oven to 180°C/350°F/Gas Mark 4, 10 minutes before baking. Lightly oil a 33 x 23 cm/13 x 9 inch baking tin. Line the base with nonstick baking parchment, oil and dust with flour.

2. Sift the first 6 ingredients into a bowl and stir in the sugars to blend. Make a well in the centre. Beat the eggs, oil and vanilla extract together and pour into the well. Using an electric mixer, gradually beat drawing in the flour mixture from the side until a smooth batter forms. Stir in the carrots, crushed pineapple and chopped nuts until blended.

3. Pour into the tin and smooth the surface evenly. Bake in the oven for 50 minutes, or until firm and a skewer inserted into the centre comes out clean. Remove from the oven. Leave to cool before removing from the tin.

4. For the frosting, beat the cream cheese, butter and vanilla extract together until smooth, then beat in the icing sugar until the frosting is smooth. Add a little milk, if necessary. Spread the frosting over the top. Refrigerate for about 1 hour to set the frosting, then cut into squares and serve.

Butterscotch Loaf

Cuts into 8 slices

1 banana, peeled, weighing about 100 g/31⁄2 oz
125 g/4 oz soft margarine
125 g/4 oz golden caster sugar
2 medium eggs
1 tsp almond extract
½ tsp vanilla extract
125 g/4 oz self-raising flour
75 g/3 oz dark chocolate chips
75 g/3 oz walnuts, chopped

To decorate:
50 g/2 oz natural icing sugar
25 g/1 oz golden lump sugar

1. Preheat the oven to 170°C/325°F/Gas Mark 3. Grease and line the base of a 1 kg/2 lb 3 oz loaf tin with a long thin strip of nonstick baking parchment.

2. Place the banana in a bowl and mash. Add the margarine, sugar and eggs along with the extracts and sift in the flour. Beat until smooth, then stir in the chocolate chips and add half the chopped walnuts. Stir until smooth, then spoon into the tin and spread level.

3. Bake for about 45 minutes until a skewer inserted into the centre comes out clean. Leave in the tin for 5 minutes, then turn out to cool on a wire rack, peel away the paper and leave to cool.

4. To decorate, make the icing sugar into a runny consistency with 2 teaspoons water. Drizzle over the cake and sprinkle over the remaining walnuts and the sugar lumps. Leave to set for 30 minutes, then serve sliced.

Banana Cake

Cuts into 8 slices

3 medium-size ripe bananas
1 tsp lemon juice
150 g/5 oz soft brown sugar
75 g/3 oz butter or margarine
250 g/9 oz self-raising flour
1 tsp ground cinnamon
3 medium eggs
50 g/2 oz walnuts, chopped
1 tsp each ground cinnamon and caster sugar, to decorate
fresh cream, to serve

1. Preheat the oven to 190°C/375°F/Gas Mark 5, 10 minutes before baking. Lightly oil and line the base of an 18 cm/ 7 inch deep round cake tin with greaseproof paper or baking parchment.

2. Mash 2 of the bananas in a small bowl, sprinkle with the lemon juice and a heaped tablespoon of the sugar. Mix together lightly and reserve.

3. Gently heat the remaining sugar and butter or margarine in a small saucepan until the butter has just melted. Pour into a small bowl, then allow to cool slightly. Sift the flour and cinnamon into a large bowl and make a well in the centre.

4. Beat the eggs into the cooled sugar mixture, pour into the well of flour, and mix thoroughly. Gently stir in the mashed banana mixture. Pour half of the mixture into the prepared tin. Thinly slice the remaining banana and arrange over the cake mixture. Sprinkle over the chopped walnuts, then cover with the remaining cake mixture. Bake in the preheated oven for 50–55 minutes, or until well risen and golden brown. Allow to cool in the tin, turn out and sprinkle with the ground cinnamon and caster sugar. Serve hot or cold with a jug of fresh cream for pouring.

Marmalade Loaf Cake

Cuts into 8–10 slices

175 g/6 oz natural golden caster sugar
175 g/6 oz butter, softened
3 medium eggs, beaten
175 g/6 oz self-raising flour
finely grated zest and juice of 1 orange
100 g/3½ oz orange marmalade

For the topping:
zest and juice of 1 orange
125 g/4 oz icing sugar

1. Preheat the oven to 180°C/350°F/Gas Mark 4. Grease and line a 1 kg/2 lb 3 oz loaf tin with a long thin strip of nonstick baking parchment.

2. Place the sugar and butter in a bowl and whisk until light and fluffy. Add the beaten egg a little at a time, adding 1 teaspoon flour with each addition.

3. Add the remaining flour to the bowl with the orange zest, 2 tablespoons orange juice and the marmalade. Using a large metal spoon, fold the mixture together using a figure-of-eight movement until all the flour is incorporated. Spoon the batter into the tin and smooth level.

4. Bake for about 40 minutes until firm in the centre and a skewer inserted into the centre comes out clean. Cool in the tin for 5 minutes, then turn out to cool on a wire rack.

5. To make the topping, peel thin strips of zest away from the orange and set aside. Squeeze the juice from the orange. Sift the icing sugar into a bowl and mix with 1 tablespoon orange juice until a thin smooth consistency forms. Drizzle over the top of the cake, letting it run down the sides. Scatter over the orange zest and leave to set for 1 hour.

Index